INTERMEDIATE LOAN

THIS ITEM MAY BE BORROWED FOR

ONE WEEK ONLY

INTERMEDIATE LOANS ARE IN HEAVY DEMAND,
PLEASE RETURN OR RENEW

To renew, tele...
01243 816089 (Bi...
01243 812099 (Bo...

D0533096

1 9 APR 2010
2 8 APR 2010
- 3 ... 2010

- 6 SEP 2010
1 4 SEP 2010

2 1 SEP 2010

- 5 OCT 2010

Trentham Books

WS 2241400 2

7 2007

First published in 1997 by Trentham Books Limited

Trentham Books Limited
Westview House
734 London Road
Oakhill
Stoke on Trent
Staffordshire
England ST4 5NP

UNIVERSITY OF CHICHESTER

© Christine Callender

All rights reserved. No part of this publication may be reproduced in any material form (including photocopying or storing it in any medium by electronic means and whether or not transiently or incidentally to some other use of this publication) without the prior written permission of the copyright owner, except in accordance with the provision of the Copyright, Designs and Patents Act 1988 or under the terms of a licence issued by the Copyright Licensing Agency, 90 Tottenham Court Road, London W1P 9HE. Applications for the Copyright owner's written permission to reproduce any part of this publication should be addressed in the first instance to the publisher.

British Cataloguing in Publication Data
A catalogue record for this book is available from the British Library
ISBN: 1 85856 072 1

Cover illustration: 'Togetherness' by Nnyanzi (1985) reproduced with the permission of Sabbokai Gallery

Designed and typeset by Trentham Print Design Ltd., Chester
and printed in Great Britain by The Cromwell Press Ltd, Wiltshire.

371 ·

i

CAL

Contents

To Ermie and Natasha

Acknowledgements

My gratitude to the staff and pupils of Stockland and Haling Park Schools (names have been changed to preserve anonymity) without whose cooperation the study would not have taken place.

I am especially indebted to Professor Viv Edwards for her immense patience, understanding, guidance and support throughout the gestation of this research.

I would also like to thank the Economic and Social Research Council (ESRC) who provided financial support in the form of a postgraduate studentship.

Last but by no means least my thanks are extended to Gillian Klein, John Eggleston and the team at Trentham Print Design.

Foreword

Why write a book about Black teachers? While debate concerning the underperformance of African Caribbean heritage children has spanned the last thirty years or so, virtually no attention has been paid to the small numbers of Black teachers in the educational system. One notable exception is Beryl Gilroy's *Black Teacher* (1976) which provided a window to the harsh realities of racism towards Black educators operating in the British education system during the 1960s.

The ensuing discussions, policy changes and research initiatives which emanated from the educational performance of African Caribbean children failed to capitalise on what was a valuable resource. Many teachers, like Gilroy, who entered the profession during this time had contributed to the success of many Black children in the Caribbean, and offered much to recent arrivals.

I was one of the lucky few who came across two Black teachers during my eleven years of compulsory schooling. Later, whilst undertaking a course of initial teacher education, I was conspicuous as one of few Black students, and certainly the only one in my chosen area of English and Drama.

My teaching career started in an inner city, predominantly White, working class area of London. It was while I worked at this school that I began to question why my colleagues would comment on my 'disciplinarian' stance and, in the next breath, refer to the good working relationships I had established with the children. It was then that I started to question whether there was something peculiar about my personality, the curriculum content or the way I taught the subject. I spoke to my colleagues and my suspicions were confirmed. I was not unique. In fact, the way I approached my work and my relationships with pupils was similar to that of my Black peers. It was through this constant quest to understand that this book evolved.

This way of looking at the experiences of Black teachers and pupils is a departure from the many studies previously undertaken in this area, and reflects personal and academic interests in documenting the lived experiences of Black educators whilst also highlighting their position in relation to the children they teach. There have been attempts to report the experiences of Black teachers in Britain but they generally tend to be concerned with the position of Black teachers and their experiences of racism. This book is quite different. It not only draws on empirical data obtained from practising Black teachers in schools but focuses particularly on the role of language in the educational context.

Like many exploratory works the book necessarily raises important questions about the experiences, practices and hopes of Black educators, questions which most Black teachers have had to ask, or are still asking themselves today. How do Black educators, for example, resolve the push-pull effects of being members of a profession which is seen to fail Black children, whilst simultaneously being members of the failing community? For some this book will challenge existing assumptions, for others it may confirm intuitions. The aim throughout is to create new ways of viewing Black teaching practices and to draw on those aspects which enhance the educational attainments of Black children.

Education for Empowerment cannot answer all these questions on its own. But, if observed within the context of a small but growing field where Black researchers are writing from new perspectives it will, I hope, bring new insights into the ways in which Black teachers are perceived and responded to within the British educational system and this will point, in turn, to new ways forward for stemming the educational derailment of Black children.

Chapter 1

Black teachers:
an endangered species?

The most recent census returns indicate that just over three million people in Britain are from ethnic minorities. People of African Caribbean heritage make up approximately thirty per cent of this group. Moreover, in comparison with the rest of the population, ethnic minorities including African Caribbeans have a relatively young profile, and it has been estimated that their number will have doubled by the year 2020 (Runnymede Trust, 1994).

Compare this with recent figures of the numbers of people from these communities applying to, and subsequently being accepted on to courses of initial teacher education. These statistics show that whilst the proportion of African Caribbean applicants is low in comparison to the population as a whole, the numbers of those who are accepted on to courses is lower still, particularly graduates. If current trends continue Black teachers are in danger of becoming an endangered species!

Traditionally, many African Caribbeans saw teaching as a route to increased status. However, their current position in the profession shows clearly that teaching is not a profession to which many young people now aspire. Although this is also true of the population as a whole, the low and ever decreasing numbers of Black teachers entering the profession is a cause for concern.

Statistical data published by both the Universities and Colleges Admissions Services (UCAS) and the Graduate Teacher Training Agency (GTTR) provide further concrete evidence that Black and ethnic minority students are under-represented in undergraduate and post-graduate courses, including those leading to teaching qualifications. Take for instance the UCAS figures for 1995, which report that Black students comprise 8 per cent of total applications for full time undergraduate and sandwich courses. Applications to education courses totalled 36,053 (0.53%) with ethnic minority applicants comprising 1,675 (4.6%).

Of these 872 (52%) were accepted. So it might appear that ethnic minority students fare well on courses of initial teacher education. These figures, however, should be viewed with caution as many of these students were mature females between the ages of 25-39 who obtained entry via an Access or Foundation course. They also tended to reside in the London area (UCAS Statistical Bulletin).

Black postgraduates too are poorly represented in teacher education courses. The GTTR collate statistics on applications, withdrawals and unplaced students for PGCE courses throughout the UK. The data show that students who identified themselves as Black Caribbean represented 0.77 per cent of applications in 1995 and 0.75 per cent of applications in 1996. (Note the high number of students placed in the 'not known' category for 1996 which may comprise a significant number of Black Caribbean students.)

Analysis of the data excluding those students in the 'not known' category point to an acceptance rate of approximately 11.5 per cent and an unplaced rate of approximately 39 per cent and whilst it is only possible to draw inferences from these figures, they do, nonetheless, point to a very low proportion of ethnic minority postgraduate students being accepted onto teaching courses. These students also tend to have higher unplaced rates than White students.

The increasingly low numbers of ethnic minority students on courses leading to teaching qualifications has prompted the Teacher Training Agency (TTA) to request that institutions pay particular attention to their recruitment procedures. Furthermore, the Office for Standards in Education (OFSTED) in their assessment of teacher training provision focus on numbers of ethic minority students as a quality assurance criterion.

Given the projected increases in minority populations in the next twenty five years, the numbers of ethnic minority teachers entering the

Table 1 Analysis of Applicants and Outcomes According to Ethnic Origin

Ethnic Origin	Acceptance				Withdrawals				Unplaced				Totals		
	M	F	T	%	M	F	T	%	M	F	T	%	M	F	T
Not Known	170	273	443	51.2	56	93	149	17.2	113	160	273	31.6	339	526	865
White	5480	10297	15777	51.4	2391	4205	6596	21.5	2994	5313	8307	27.1	10865	19815	30680
Black Caribbean	31	81	112	42.6	12	35	47	17.9	26	78	104	39.5	69	194	263
Black African	59	69	128	29.5	35	30	65	15.0	114	127	241	55.5	208	226	434
Black Other	13	42	55	52.9	1	13	14	13.5	13	22	35	33.7	27	77	104
Asian Indian	96	193	289	47.2	50	69	119	19.4	58	146	204	33.3	204	408	612
Asian Pakistani	82	109	191	47.9	27	44	71	17.8	65	72	137	34.3	174	225	399
Asian Bangladeshi	23	24	47	43.9	5	9	14	13.1	22	24	46	43.0	50	57	107
Asian Chinese	14	18	32	42.1	8	12	20	26.3	8	16	24	31.6	30	46	76
Asian Other	56	79	135	46.6	17	36	53	18.3	50	52	102	35.2	123	167	290
Total	6024	11185	17209	50.9	2602	4546	7148	21.1	3463	6010	9473	28.0	12089	21741	33830

M = Male   F = Female   T = Total

Source: Graduate Teacher Training Registry (1995)

Table 2 Analysis of Applicants and Outcomes According to Ethnic Origin

Ethnic Origin	Acceptance				Withdrawals				Unplaced				Totals		
	M	F	T	%	M	F	T	%	M	F	T	%	M	F	T
Not Known	753	1389	2142	50.0	264	492	756	17.7	499	883	1382	32.3	1516	2764	4280
White	5247	10084	15331	55.4	1912	3380	5292	19.1	2373	4700	7073	25.5	9532	18164	37696
Black Caribbean	31	91	122	47.8	11	34	45	17.6	25	63	88	34.5	67	188	255
Black African	72	59	131	35.3	35	39	74	19.9	71	95	166	44.7	178	193	371
Black Other	10	26	36	40.4	4	17	21	23.6	9	23	32	36.0	23	66	89
Asian Indian	70	161	231	45.9	31	58	89	17.7	40	143	183	36.4	141	362	503
Asian Pakistani	63	111	174	49.0	36	40	76	21.4	38	67	105	29.6	137	218	355
Asian Bangladeshi	23	32	47	43.9	9	10	19	17.1	16	21	37	33.3	48	63	111
Asian Chinese	11	23	34	43.0	9	18	27	34.2	3	15	18	22.8	23	56	79
Asian Other	36	40	76	42.0	11	16	27	14.9	32	46	78	43.1	79	102	181
Total	6316	12016	18332	54.0	2322	4104	6426	18.9	3106	6056	9162	27.0	11744	22176	33920

M = Male F = Female T = Total

Source: Graduate Teacher Training Registry (1996)

teaching profession is a matter which requires urgent attention at local, national and policy levels. But only if there are concerted efforts on the part of those involved in the education of minority pupils will the numbers of ethnic minority teachers be increased.

The context

The study then, was borne out of wider concerns involving the education of Black children, the low numbers of Black teachers in the profession and the experiences of pupils and teachers in the school setting. It involves six Black and two White teachers in two primary schools. The primary sector was chosen because many research studies on ethnic minority attainment have indicated patterns which suggest African Caribbean children fall behind at an early stage of their educational careers (see for example, Mabey, 1981; Scarr et al, 1983; Tizard et al, 1988).

In concentrating primarily on Black educators it was important to select schools where Black teachers were sufficiently represented. To this end, contact was made with Advisers from the local education authority to find schools which comprised at least forty per cent African Caribbean teaching staff and a pupil population reflecting the diversity of the teaching personnel. Seven schools matched the criteria and each was contacted by letter of introduction. A short time later, headteachers were contacted by telephone to discuss the project further and to arrange an appointment. Three schools then declined as the period of data collection coincided with teaching practice and they felt that the presence of a researcher would create unacceptable additional stress. The remaining schools were visited and eventually two were chosen. The schools, Stockland and Haling Park, offered viable numbers of teachers prepared to take part in the study. The six Black and two White teachers who took part were chosen on the basis of their willingness to participate and for no other reason.

The children (of whom there were two hundred and eleven in total) were aged between five and eleven years of age. It is recognised that it would have been preferable to focus on a narrower age range. It is highly probable, for instance, that the perceptions of older children might well be different from younger children and so too might be their ability to articulate their feelings. The age range, however, was again a function of teacher willingness to take part in the study.

Stockland School

Stockland, a large two form entry school, is situated in the north of the borough, surrounded by a range of local authority housing. Many of the children who attend Stockland are drawn from the local area. The ethnic origins of the pupils are mirrored, to some extent, in the staffing of the school. For example, African Caribbean pupils represent fifty one per cent of the student population and of a total of nineteen teachers, eleven are of African Caribbean origin. African Caribbean teachers are found at all levels within the school including the headteacher, deputy head and curriculum co-ordinators. Three teachers and seventy eight pupils from Stockland took part in the study.

Adebola Adesanya is of Nigerian origin and at the time of the study had been teaching at Stockland for four years. After several years teaching in mission schools in West Africa she came to the UK to continue her studies. Adebola teaches years five and six.

Evadne Sargeant has taught at Stockland for two and a half years. She has many years experience of teaching in Guyana where she was a headteacher. On entering the teaching profession in Britain Evadne was required to retrain in order to gain qualified teacher status (QTS) because her qualifications from the Caribbean were not recognised. She therefore had to undergo an eighteen month probationary period in order to fulfil the requirements of the Licensed Teachers Scheme. Evadne teaches year one.

Lastly, Deborah Lashley is a Black British teacher of Barbadian/ Jamaican heritage. She has taught at Stockland since qualifying as a teacher three years earlier. Deborah teachers years three and four.

Haling Park School

Haling Park is a single form entry school situated in the east of the borough. Its catchment area encompasses a large number of council and privately owned properties and, again, many of the pupils are drawn from the locality. The pupil and staff populations of Haling Park are reflective of the local community as a whole, and African Caribbean staff are represented at senior management and other levels.

One hundred and thirty three pupils from Haling Park took part in the study. So did three Black teachers from Haling Park. Winston Thompson is Jamaican and has many years experience of teaching in various settings, including primary, secondary, tertiary and higher education. He has taught at Haling Park for five years and teaches years five and six.

Leroy Wiltshire, from Trinidad, was recruited under the same scheme as Evadne Sargeant. He taught in Trinidadian secondary schools for fifteen years before joining Haling Park, where he has taught for two and a half years. He currently teaches years five and six.

Pearlette Campbell comes from Jamaica and has been teaching at Haling Park for two years. She taught for six years in convent schools before teaching in the UK. Pearlette teaches years three and four.

Initially consideration was given to a matched sample of Black teachers and White but the large number of variables to be considered (eg. age, gender, teaching experience etc) made this impractical. Lessons with four White teachers were observed, two in each school, as a way of exploring general ethos and the extent to which whole school policy was evident in the organisation of both Black teachers and White. Later however, two teachers at Stockland withdrew, one because of long term illness and the other due to uncertainties about the video-recorded aspects of the data collection. The two remaining teachers are Peter James and Sarah Brown.

Peter James is a New Zealander and has been teaching for eleven years, both in New Zealand and the UK. Peter currently works with years one and two and has been teaching at Haling Park for two years.

Sarah Brown is White British and joined Haling Park immediately after graduating from teacher training college. She teaches years three and four.

Although it is clearly inappropriate to generalise from such small samples, the observation of Peter and Sarah has sometimes made it possible to compare the reactions of Black teachers and White to similar situations and to speculate on whether these behaviours might be more widespread.

Methodology

The study was undertaken within the ethnographic tradition. This method of research is concerned 'with the meaning of actions and events to the people we seek to understand' (Spradley, 1974). Thus, central to the ethnographic pursuit is the relationship between the researcher and those being researched, a characteristic which is neatly captured by Hammersley and Atkinson (1991:2) who argue that the ethnographer

> ... participates, either overtly or covertly, in people's daily lives for an extended period of time, watching what happens, listening to what is said, asking questions; in fact collecting whatever data are available to throw light on the issues with which he or she is concerned.

A key factor in ethnography is that of reflexivity, that is, acknowledging that we are part of the social world we study. This also involves recognising that, in all social research, there is a reliance on common sense knowledge and common sense methods of investigation.

Ethnography also relies on a number of data collection techniques which allow for the systematic comparison of data. A range of checks, therefore, may be incorporated into the research process in order to aid verification and rigour in data collection and analysis.

Traditional ethnography such as that described above, however, has been criticised on a number of fronts. It has been argued, for instance, that ethnography relies on anecdotal evidence which supports the researchers' point of view (Watson-Gegeo, 1988). These claims have been challenged on the basis that representative data which reflects typicality and variation may go some way towards alleviating this problem (Werner and Schoepfle, 1987).

Another criticism of traditional ethnography is that it is concerned primarily with description and analysis. As a consequence, writers have suggested that it misses valuable opportunities to challenge the status quo (Cazden, 1983; Lather, 1986). Critical ethnography, on the other hand, has the potential to effect change. Simon and Dippo (1986:196) argue that critical ethnography has

> ... neither a neutral nor arbitrary interest. Rather, it is an interest organised by a stand-point which implicates us in moral questions about desirable forms of social relations and ways of living. Thus the interest that defines critical ethnographers is both pedagogical and political.

Thus whilst traditional ethnography is concerned with what is, critical ethnography aims to describe what could be. Unlike traditional ethnography which 'speaks for' those being researched, critical ethnography creates an audience for informants and this, in turn, acts a means of empowerment.

By its very nature critical ethnography raises issues of researcher bias but, as Simon and Dippo observe, this is no more of a problem than to those using qualitative or quantitative approaches. Instead, they view

> ... all forms of knowing and all particular knowledge forms as ideological, hence the issue is not whether one is 'biased'; but rather, whose interests are served by one's work (p. 196).

A range of in-built checking mechanisms was therefore adopted, including

- triangulation, both methodological and data orientated (Woods, 1990)

- respondent validation – the requirement that informants are visited on a number of occasions and in a variety of settings in order to validate their claims (Hammersley and Atkinson, 1991)

- reflexive subjectivity – the importance of recognising one's personal values and ideologies affect the research process (Thomas, 1993). Accordingly, I have offered an outline of my personal interests and assumptions on the topic

- finally, catalytic validity, which requires that documentation of the research project should lead to a greater awareness and, where possible, the increased participation of informants. This has taken a number of forms including informal discussion, dissemination through staff development and now the publication of this book.

Data collection

The main data collection for this study took place over six months and employed a range of data collection techniques. Fieldnotes which were kept for each teacher during the early stages of observation and proved indispensable in providing supplementary information on a number of topics.

I also made observations of day-to-day classroom activity and had a certain fluidity in my role – for much of the time I aimed to be a non-participant observer (Walker, 1990; Woods, 1991) but at other times I was seen as another adult who could be called upon case of emergency, a sympathetic colleague or a trusted intimate to whom teachers and headteachers could turn. At all times I was aware of 'the observer's paradox', that is the effect that the presence of the researcher has upon the behaviour of those being researched. However, discussions held later with teachers indicate that my presence had little effect on the daily activities of the classroom.

Tape and video-recorded data also formed a part of data collection. Given the number of activities which may be taking place in a classroom at any given moment, it is very difficult to collect good quality data. Recording what happens as it happens is a way of overcoming this difficulty (Mehan, 1993). So after an initial observation period, the teachers were video-recorded for a period of four days each and wore radio-microphones to enhance sound quality. Pupils and parents were also forewarned that recording would take place; this, it was hoped, would limit the potentially disruptive presence of the video-recorder and give parents the opportunity to withdraw their children if they so wished.

Teachers and pupils were interviewed, each teacher on at least two occasions, and when necessary for follow-up meetings which mostly took place out of school hours. Teachers were asked about previous teaching experiences, their views on Black underperformance and about the strategies they used when teaching Black children. The children, on the other hand, were interviewed only once, in single sex groups of four. All interviews took place during school hours in the library. Pupils were asked about their perceptions of school and teachers and about their future aspirations.

Whilst it would have been advantageous to interview pupils at a later stage of the research, the practical considerations involved were too great. For example, some children who had been in year six at the time of data collection had, in fact, left soon after they were interviewed. Additionally, some children had changed class, making it extremely difficult to coordinate the interviews because of the larger number of people now involved.

Insider research

I am sure that my position as a Black female researcher enabled me to gain several perspectives on the topic under investigation. I was able to observe the teaching context without being an active participant. My experience as a teacher also enabled me to interpret the day-to-day activities from an educational perspective. Finally, my ethnicity gave me more rapid access to data which might have eluded a White researcher working on the same subject over the same period.

Having a similar ethnic background has both advantages and disadvantages. For example, shared ethnicity can open doors to meanings normally reserved for ingroup members. However, it is also possible that doors may be closed as the researcher becomes too immersed in the situation to see clearly what is happening (Hill-Collins, 1986). In order to safeguard against this possibility, respondent validation and triangulation acted as checking mechanisms in the research process.

The role of Black researchers in education

The debate on Black participation in educational research is not new (see for instance, Constantine-Simms, 1995) and Black researchers have traditionally been excluded from the research process. When they have been involved, it has usually been as the vehicle through which some White researchers have obtained information about the Black community. This has led to mixed results. On the one hand, there has been a plethora of studies which have relied on Black fieldworkers but still, unsurprisingly, promulgate eurocentric perspectives. But the vital issues of race and ethnic minority achievement are now being researched by a small number of Black researchers offering their perspectives. This is not to suggest that the number of Black researchers currently working in the field is commensurate with the enormity of the task. Rather, it points to exclusionary practices which are ever present in the domain of academic research. Furthermore, definitive action is needed if there is to be any change.

The structure of the book

The early chapters of the book provide the backdrop to the discussion which follows. Chapter two reviews a range of minority perspectives for the underperformance of Black pupils in British and American schools, focusing on issues such as culture and caste, learning styles, effective teachers, community nomination and achievement studies and under achieving gifted Black pupils.

Chapter three explores the language of Caribbean heritage children in British schools. Specific reference is made to the current linguistic situation of Black British children and the implications of recent changes to educational legislation are explored.

The position of Black teachers and pupils is considered in chapter four. The discussion highlights the ways in which culture manifests itself in the educational context and considers the differential treatment of enthic minority children in multi-ethnic classrooms. It then goes on to explore differences in cultural style and the ways in which it can affect teacher-pupil interaction. Finally it considers coping and survival strategies and the position of Black pedagogues in British schools.

Chapter five describes a range of retained African verbal and non-verbal communication patterns found amongst six Black teachers who form the focus of this study. It looks particularly at their use of: call-response, repetition, proverbial expression, moral teachings, body language, oculesic and paralinguistic features, drawing on examples of teacher behaviour observed during fieldwork.

One of the most important areas of difference between Black teachers and White appears to lie in their use of rewarding and reprimanding strategies. In chapter six attention is focused on Black teachers' use of praise and blame and reasons are put forward to explain the ways in which Black teachers' regulatory behaviour is emancipatory in intent, reflecting a desire that Black pupils reach their full potential.

Chapter seven explores the role which gender plays in this process. A discussion of gender issues in classroom interaction, and ethnic and gender stereotypes, form the backdrop for an analysis of Black teacher reward and reprimanding behaviour across four dyads.

In chapter eight the main findings of the research are summarised and various themes which have emerged are drawn together. The implications of the study are considered and further avenues for research are highlighted.

Chapter 2

Research from a Black perspective

The underperformance of Black children in the British educational system has been, and still is, a cause for concern. In recent years a growing body of research has been undertaken by Black writers or by others anxious to explore Black perspectives on educational underperformance. This research is in the 'interpretative' tradition, which asserts that minority groups should be encouraged to find their own solutions to underachievement rather than allowing majority group specialists to do so for them. The research has tended to be more holistic in approach than many earlier studies of achievement, concentrating on the nature of Black experience rather than on comparisons of educational outcomes for different groups of children. It has focused, for instance, on issues such as culture and caste and differences in learning styles. It has also pointed to methodological innovations such as 'community nomination', which have considerable potential in the development of educational achievement.

Culture and Caste
In an attempt to address equal opportunity in education, anthropologists have proposed that schools are agents of cultural transmission, arenas of cultural conflict, and potential sites of micro and macro level change (Spindler, 1988). Whereas early attempts to explain the underperformance of Black children tended to pathologise the issue, more recent explanations have shifted to an exploration of ways in which the culture of the school is failing to meet the needs of ethnic minority children

(see, for instance, Mohatt and Erickson, 1981; Au and Jordan, 1981 and Mascias, 1987).

The interpretative tradition argues that educational responses to underachievement need to be more analytical and reflective, allowing groups to construct their own social histories. Writers who support the view claim that critical theory offers inadequate explanation, since it is 'experts' from the dominant culture who guide the education of ethnic minority groups. Even though the changes recommended by the experts may be in the interests of the group concerned, these groups have little influence on the direction of these changes. Both functionalist and critical approaches, it is argued, are useful in terms of providing generalised observations, but are too far removed from the day-to-day experiences of ethnic minority groups to provide meaningful explanations. Interpretative research, however, aims to overcome these criticisms by encouraging minority participation in the investigation of minority group underachievement. Schools are regarded as social constructs that operate within a larger power structure. Building on critical theory, interpretative responses to education promote a pluralistic approach which makes the minority community the focus of investigation. The ethnic revitalisation and tolerance for cultural pluralism that may result are useful in providing more relevant and equal educational provision.

The work of Ogbu (1974; 1978; 1981;1987) and, more recently, Gibson and Ogbu (1991) have been particularly important in sharpening perceptions of the ways in which education is moulded by society. Gibson and Ogbu (1991), for instance, propose that the traditional explanation of ethnic minority underachievement has failed to consider the perspectives of the groups themselves. Instead they argue that the dominant group has

> ... evaluated the behaviours of minorities from the perspective of the dominant group's perceptions of their own social reality or from the perceptions and interpretations that the dominant group members have of their own social reality of minorities (p. 6).

Because traditional explanations have often regarded minority groups as homogenous entities, Gibson and Ogbu (1991) suggest that they are unable to explain the variability that exists between different groups.

Ogbu (1987) divides minorities into two groups: immigrant and involuntary minorities. Immigrant minorities, are, according to Ogbu, those who have migrated to the host society on a voluntary basis. They arrive with strong cultural and social identities and do not regard educational ideology as threatening their cultural distinctiveness. They function outside of the dominant social structure and hold attitudes that allow them to accept and expect prejudice and discrimination more readily as the price of achieving their objectives. Although immigrant minorities are often found in the lower social strata and have little political or economic power, they do not necessarily regard themselves as being inferior. Additionally, such groups have the option of returning to their homeland or relocating to another society. In general, their goal is not equality. Instead, they are concerned with improving their economic position relative to that in their country of origin.

Involuntary minority groups, on the other hand, do not generally have a homeland with which to compare their situation, and, as a result, are forced to make comparisons with the dominant group. Such a comparison reinforces their subordinate status, which is seen by the group as a permanent condition. Further, their inferior position can only be challenged through collective resistance over an extended time. Involuntary groups regard the dominant educational ideology as a form of 'cultural genocide'. Collaboration with and acceptance of such ideals represents an alliance with those who have traditionally oppressed minority groups. According to Gibson and Ogbu, the failure of large numbers of minority students can be attributed to the belief that their efforts will not be recognised in terms of the types of employment they will be offered and the social recognition that is granted to them. Consequently, they associate the acquisition of the dominant language and culture with those who have traditionally oppressed them. The dominant group generally regards involuntary groups as inferior in every respect and prevents them from competing for the most desirable positions on the basis of their individual training and ability. The positions that they are forced to hold reinforce and perpetuate the belief that they are more suited to the low-status positions in society. Their political dependence is thus guaranteed through their economic subordination.

Immigrant and involuntary minorities may differ from the dominant group in terms of language, cultural and social identities. However, the quality of these differences can vary for each group. This qualitative difference, Ogbu (1987) argues, can affect the way in which minority group children perceive and respond to the process of schooling. He divides differences into primary and secondary cultural differences. Primary cultural differences, he claims, are found in immigrant groups and existed before they came in to contact with the dominant society. Secondary cultural differences are those which arise after two populations have come into continuous contact or after members of a given group have participated in an institution (ie school) controlled by another group. Ogbu cites Black Americans as a group displaying secondary cultural differences, and claims that the experience of slavery forced many Blacks in America to develop alternative cultural ways of coping, feeling and perceiving in relation to White Americans. He argues that there are specific features of secondary cultural differences, such as style, that should be noted, as they not only have particular relevance to the experiences of minority groups and schooling, but also have significance to educational anthropologists who try to explain the behaviours of these children.

An understanding of the varying aspirations and orientations of minority groups has obvious implications for the study of differential educational performance. Although Ogbu's analysis has been criticised from various perspectives (cf Erickson, 1987; McDermott, 1987; Foley, 1991; Baker, 1993), it offers a useful framework for interpreting the achievements of minority groups in the UK, the USA and elsewhere. It has also prepared the way for a wide range of studies which explore the mismatch between the cultural background of minority students and the teaching styles to which they are exposed in schools.

Learning Styles

Another attempt to explain the underperformance of minority students from a minority perspective has been through the study of learning styles. The discussion of learning styles has a long history. Klein (1951), for instance, proposes two main kinds of students: '*levelers*' whose perception and judgement tend to be fixed and who are reluctant to change their views even when presented with new evidence or changing conditions; and '*sharpeners*' who are attuned to change and capable of spotting shades of difference. In a similar vein, Kagan (1964) draws attention to the degree to which the learner reflects on the validity of alternative solutions; while Ausubel (1968) distinguishes between *satellizers* who have an inherent sense of self-worth independent of what they accomplish, and *non-satellizers* who lack such self-worth and feel it necessary to prove themselves through their accomplishments. Witkin (1962) and Witkin et al (1977) make a distinction between *field dependence* and *field independence*: field dependent learners rely on environmental support while field independent learners are restricted by the situations in which they find themselves.

Domino (1971) looks at the implications of learning styles for the class-room. He explores, for instance, how a personality trait could be used to select an optimal instructional approach. Such a line of inquiry, how-ever, has proved problematic. Cronbach and Snow (1977), for instance, find no evidence that students with particular personality traits respond better to teachers who hold corresponding personality traits.

The discussion of learning styles has also been extended to different cultural and ethnic groups. Ramirez and Casteneda (1974), for example, adapted Witkin's field-dependent/field-independent typology as a means of explaining the disparity between Latino and Anglo school performance. Additionally, Cohen (1969) observed that minority students prefer relational styles whereas schools generally favour and reward analytical modes. Writers like Shade (1982) and Hale-Benson (1986) have applied the concept of learning styles to the needs of Black students in America. Shade, for instance, observes that the culture and lifestyles of African-Americans are based on strategies that promote survival and which tend to be universalistic, intuitive and person-orientated. This is in direct contrast to the American education system which requires cognitive strategies that are sequential, analytical and object orientated. The result is that such polar differences can work to the detriment of African-American students.

Studies of learning styles are open to criticism on a number of levels. Firstly, only a few styles (field dependence/independence, reflection/impulsivity) have been extensively studied. Secondly, this research is rarely linked to teachers' learning or teaching styles. Finally, and perhaps most importantly in terms of ethnic minority performance, is the fact that there is little evidence to suggest that distinguishing students according to learning style makes any significant difference to their academic performance. As Hilliard (1989) points out, style has been used as an excuse for both the low expectations of teachers and second-rate teaching methods. While acknowledging that style is cultural (or learned) and important in teaching and learning, he disputes the notion that pedagogy should be modified in response to learning styles.

Effective Black teachers

There is a growing body of research that concentrates on the knowledge and skills required to 'effectively' teach minority pupils. This has taken two distinct but closely related routes: studies which focus on the extent to which teachers exhibit culturally identifiable techniques in their educational practice; and teacher education programs suitable for teachers working with culturally diverse students. Burstein and Cabello (1989) for example, concentrate on the development of teacher education. They examine the effect of a teacher education programme which aims to increase the cultural awareness of the teachers who will be working with 'culturally diverse' students. They found that, after two years, teachers who had completed the programme showed significant changes in their attitudes towards and knowledge of culturally diverse students. In short, the teachers' practice had been affected by exposure to a programme that made explicit the nature of culturally diverse students. The extent to which these findings could be related to student achievement, however, was not considered and Burstein and Cabello acknowledge the need for further research in this area.

The question of culturally different teaching styles offers an even more interesting line of inquiry and studies of teachers have been extensive. However, they have generally failed to highlight the practice of Black teachers, concentrating rather on the underachievement of Black children and attributing failure to their families and socio-economic status. The majority of those which have concentrated on Black teachers have portrayed them as insensitive, authoritarian individuals, upholders of the status-quo who are ill-suited to teaching Black students effectively. Rist (1970) for example, in an observational study of Black kindergarten and second-grade teachers reported that children were divided into 'ideal' types by the Black teachers. This categorisation, he claimed, was based on criteria such as physical appearance, which included cleanliness of clothes, body odour, condition of hair and 'Blackness' of skin. Additionally, he suggests that the placement of children into reading groups which reflected social class during the early years of schooling, and the teachers' behaviour towards the children were important influences on eventual attainment.

Rist's observations may well underline the fact that some Black teachers are not successful with Black students. They should, however, be viewed with some caution. Throughout his discussion he makes generalisations not only about the children he observes but, more importantly, he assumes knowledge about the cultural identities of the teachers involved in the study. Rist's preoccupation with placing Black female teachers into a White middle-class cultural framework means that his conclusions frequently mirror those of the dominant group in American society. References to the 'irrational' nature of teacher decisions and the presence of 'attitudinal and behavioural characteristics' in the children would appear to be examples of his preconceived notions about Black children and Black teachers.

There are nevertheless, a few exceptions to this trend. Lightfoot (1973) for instance, considers the political and social ideologies of two Black teachers. She found evidence of a 'hidden curriculum' which sought to empower and educate Black students. The teachers in her study represented divergent belief and value systems and they also held different ideas about what constituted school success. For the greater part, however, American studies have failed to consider the effects of racial identity on the belief systems of teachers. This is despite growing evidence which suggests that the previous life experiences, background, identity, culture and critical incidents in teachers' lives help shape their teaching practice (Goodson, 1992).

A particularly important development in research on Black teachers is the introduction of community nomination, whereby an 'insider's' perspective is sought as a means of identifying 'effective' teachers of minority pupils (M. Foster, 1989, 1990, 1991). The significance of community nomination as a methodological tool is that it seeks to explore the perceptions of the Black community, a perspective which has almost invariably been overlooked in research in this area undertaken by White academics. Teachers nominated in this way have been found to display certain well-defined characteristics. They exhibit cultural solidarity with their students. They take responsibility for teaching the knowledge, skills and values that facilitate school success, self-determination, healthy cultural identity and survival in a society that professes equal opportunity while practising institutional racism. They link classroom content to students' out-of-school experience. They use familiar cultural patterns to organise classroom interaction. Finally, they incorporate culturally familiar communication patterns into classroom activities. It is acknowledged that similar background does not, of course, guarantee school success, nor do good working relationships between teacher and pupil. Some teachers may, in fact, judge students more harshly because they remind them of their former selves.

Cazden (1988), drawing on sociolinguistic and ethnographic research, argues that some of the most effective schooling takes place where cultural solidarity and power are combined. In situations where students and teachers share a common cultural background and where they are able to engage in productive interactions, students may be motivated to perform educationally in ways that they otherwise might not. The sense of cultural solidarity can be implicit and unspoken where the teachers are recognised members of the reference group. Or it may be may be explicit and continuously reinforced in classroom interaction.

Research which examines the practices of effective Black teachers has found that such teachers have strong attachments to the Black community and report themselves as being of it. Ladson-Billings and Henry (1990), for instance, observed the pedagogical strategies of thirteen successful teachers of Black students in an ethnographic study in the USA and Canada. The teachers who formed the focus for the study were contacted through 'community nomination' and were from culturally diverse backgrounds. Ladson-Billings and Henry (1990) conclude that

> ... successful teachers of Black students have a positive perspective about the role and use of African culture in teaching students and recognise that they work in opposition to the very school systems that employ them (p.84).

They also report that 'teachers regularly use methods that draw upon the students' African cultural roots to help students succeed' (p. 79).

'Connectedness' – the presence of strong kinship bonds and a sense of mutual obligation – is also evidenced in the practice of effective Black teachers (Lyons, 1983; M. Foster, 1991). (For a discussion of similar issues in Hispanic classrooms see Cazden, 1988 and Garcia and Otheguy, 1991.) This is not to suggest that Black teachers are overly permissive, nor as, some scholars have suggested, that Black mothers are unnecessarily authoritarian and controlling (Rist, 1970). What is apparent is that their style closely resembles the authoritative parenting style where acceptance and involvement are integrated with firm control and personal autonomy. Consequently, when Black teachers take on the role of kin they invariably embrace a complex set of behaviours that demand appropriate attention to firmness and nurture.

Effective teachers ensure that classroom content, too, is linked to student experiences and students are encouraged to bring community experiences into the classroom (M. Foster, 1989; Ladson-Billings, 1990; Ladson-Billings and Henry, 1990). They are also concerned with the development of children – not just their cognitive growth but also their social and emotional growth – and their practice reflects this commitment. Effective Black teachers accept responsibility for nurturing in their students the skills necessary for success in school, and values such as persistence and responsibility which serve as a foundation to current and future learning. They foster student interests and are also aware of the structural inequalities in society. Thus, their practice is influenced by a 'hidden curriculum' of self-determination which is designed to help students cope with the reality of living in an unequal society.

While anthropological research suggests that the Black community has maintained the cultural values of equality, and collective responsibility in many areas, including literacy (Heath, 1983), most of what occurs in traditional classrooms encourages competitive behaviour and individual achievement. Effective Black teachers, however, encourage cultural patterns of collectivity, incorporating them into everyday classroom activities. Students are not only encouraged to work together but also to support each other and to study collaboratively. Ladson-Billings (1991), for instance, reports that many of the teachers she interviewed stressed the need to build 'a community or family' and that both they and the students felt comfortable working in cooperative and collaborative classrooms. (See Au (1980) and Dumont (1972) for discussion of similar issues in relation to Hawaiian and Cherokee classrooms respectively).

Heath's (1983) research adds weight to arguments for the importance of acknowledging cultural differences in the classroom. She examined language use and learning in Trackton, a Black community, in North Carolina and then incorporated some of the interactional features into the classroom. Her findings demonstrate that reducing the socio-linguistic discontinuity between students' home and school environments can positively influence Black students' participation in school lessons.

In addition to interactional style, effective Black teachers often incorporate aspects of Black communicative patterns into classroom events. Hollins (1982), for instance, undertakes an analysis of Marva Collins, founder of Westside Prep (a school well known for its high rate of achievement with minority pupils). She found evidence of Black communicative behaviour in Collins' teaching style, including participation patterns such as call-and-response and use of analogies and rhythm.

Other researchers have also alluded to the use of familiar communicative patterns in classroom activity. Ladson-Billings and Henry (1990) report that rhythms, call-and-response and the use of proverbs characterised the pedagogy of the effective Black teachers they studied. Finally, in a sociolinguistic analysis of a successful Black teacher, Foster (1989), found evidence of code-switching between the teacher's more standard English, used for regulatory purposes, and the Black expressive speech found in sermons and raps (labelled 'performances' in this study), used almost exclusively during academic tasks. In many cases, the use of Black expressive language, manipulation of metaphors and code-switching into familiar Black English patterns is a conscious and deliberate choice made by the teacher (M. Foster, 1989; Ladson-Billings and Henry, 1990).

Achievement studies and gifted Black pupils

Recent work in Britain and the USA has focused, unlike previous research, on Black pupils in positive classrooms and gifted Black students who are underachieving. Whilst these research studies have used small sample sizes they do, nonethelesss, provide useful starting points for new and fresh perspectives to the problem of under-achievement. Nehaul (1996) for instance, observed the classrooms of five teachers (four female and one male) across four schools in an effort to ascertain the factors which contribute towards the achievement of Black children. No specific references are made to teacher ethnicity. Schools were selected after consultation with specialist advisory staff and advisers who perceived them 'as being more 'positive' i.e. genuinely interested in ensuring that equal opportunities are available for their Black pupils' (p. 50). Additional criteria included the presence of Black teachers and/or headteachers and schools with significant numbers of Caribbean pupils and those with fewer Caribbean children on roll.

Underlying Nehaul's approach to the study is the contention that previous research has focused on racist or 'less aware' teachers. She argues that, by focusing on those at the opposite end of this continuum, i.e. those who are non-racist and 'more aware', it may be possible to isolate the practices, circumstances and conditions which lead to improved/increased attainments amongst Caribbean children.

Nehaul proposes a pastoral model, identifying key factors which contribute to successful achievement of Caribbean pupils. These include pupil characteristics, classroom ethos, teacher perceptions of the factors contributing to achievement amongst Caribbean pupils and parental involvement. She notes, for example, that teachers did not perceive race and children's backgrounds as significant in their success. Rather, teachers felt it was important to use a number of strategies ranging from focusing on individual student need, providing appropriate and challenging tasks; to ensuring that children's backgrounds were an integral part of the curriculum, using a range of resources including parents and multicultural materials; to monitoring progress and treating all children equally.

She observed a number of high and low achieving children, and her descriptions of these children are particularly illuminating. She writes, for example, of pupils one and two, who are regarded as pupils who have 'had negative experiences at school because they were Black and of Caribbean heritage' (p. 119). Pupil one, for instance, is 'very clever, advanced in reading and maths, but not articulate and as yet without the interpersonal and communication skills for making and enjoying friendships' (p. 120). Yet, in her analysis Nehaul alludes to 'something in the child's body language' which led her to believe that she was being weighed up. She concludes that:

while being in the classroom was a generally positive experience for this pupil, being Black added a very real and negative dimension that reduced confidence ... it seemed to me that achievement was and would continue to be affected (p. 121).

Later, Nehaul recounts her observations of another child, pupil eight. She observes that:

... in the classroom she would work at a table with the same three close friends – all White ... In the playground, the child would usually be with one or more of these friends ... Although Pupil Eight's closest friends appeared to be these White pupils, when the children lined up. When coming from assembly to class for example, the child always came in with at least two of the other Black pupils, not necessarily the same ones, and she also clustered with other Black pupils in the playground in spite of the relatively small proportion at the school' (p. 127).

Unfortunately, closer analysis of Nehaul's research demonstrates that she is in danger of recreating and affirming the same imbalance she claims to overturn (p. 49). The absence of any information relating to her own or the teachers' ethnicity is a weakness, considering the nature of the topic and the already established research literature which looks at issues such as these. Another equally important element is Nehaul's analysis and subsequent interpretation of extracts similar to those cited above. Here it may be argued that she shows limited understanding of communication in the Black idiom (for further discussion see chapter five) and alludes to the possibility that, for pupil one, being Black is a possible indicator of underachievement (cf. Ford, 1995). Furthermore, she fails to explore the notion that Pupil Eight may, in fact, be adopting the use of pragmatic strategies of the type observed amongst high achieving children (cf. Fordham and Ogbu, 1986; Fordham, 1988).

Channer (1996), on the other hand, uses the life history method to investigate the factors which contribute to the success of her high achieving respondents. Twelve participants between the ages of 25-40 years, all of whom were graduates, were interviewed in order to identify the factors which contributed to or impeded their success. Additionally, they were required to have received some of their education in the UK. Most were regular attenders at church or had been in the past.

Several themes emerged which were identified as having an effect on the respondents' eventual outcomes. Many spoke of their early education in Britain and pointed to a range of school experiences which impacted upon their progress and subsequent achievement. School experiences were mixed but those who attended school in the Caribbean felt that this put them in a strong position where 'they were less likely to internalise inferior, racist or oppressive views' (p. 73). Not all experiences of British schooling were negative, however, and it was not unusual for pupils to be 'sponsored' by interested teachers who helped them to develop their academic abilities. Linguistic concerns were also an issue and centred, for instance, on teachers who focused attention not on the grammatical correctness of students' work (which was often well in advance of their peers'), but instead on matters of pronunciation. This often meant that although respondents felt a strong sense of pride in their Creole languages they were undermined by the actions of their teachers. The role of sport, racism, positive role models, a strong sense of family values, parental awareness and involvement, experiences and access to higher education, lack of supportive and/or relevant careers and academic guidance and experiences in the workplace also contributed to the shaping of these individuals and their academic success.

The one factor which remained constant in the lives of the respondents however, was their current or past commitment to the church and religion in general. Several key factors emerge as significant. Self discipline, for example, helped them in potentially difficult situations. Coupled with this was the need for respondents to be seen as 'good pupils'. Several also commented that regular attendance at church provided them with a strong personal, social and community identity. One respondent spoke of his determination to succeed academically despite being 'knocked, dented and de-skilled'. The high degree of commitment and resilience demonstrated by the participants was related to their strong sense of purpose and direction, along with personal motivation which was sometimes a response to the negative views and expectations of others. For many, adolescence and young adulthood brought about a period of doubt, raising questions relating to early upbringing and continued participation in the church. As one would expect, this period often coincided with a growth in political awareness. Again, responses varied: some rebelled against parents and religion whilst others reaffirmed and nurtured their relationship with God and the church.

What is clear from Channer's study, however, is the very strong impact that religious affiliation had on the participants. The combination of these factors, particularly the support and security of the church, contributed towards promoting a strong achievement ethic. Which, in this case, undoubtedly attributed to the successes of these Black achievers.

Channer's work also points to a range of institutionalised practices prevalent at the time, and which to some extent exist today. These include teachers' reluctance to communicate to Black parents the exact status of their children's academic ability until it is too late and the 'marking down' of Black students when they write about issues of concern to them, often due to a lack of 'academic rigour' (cf. ref).

Ford (1995), reporting on the underachievement of gifted Black students, explores the factors which lead to poor representation of Black students in gifted programs. She investigates the degree to which students' learning contexts, peer relations, sense of fairness, parental achievements, racial identities, anxiety levels and their sense of responsibility for their personal behaviour, learning and achievement affected their academic performance. One hundred and fifty two middle and high school students took part in the study (97 female and 55 male), many of whom reported that they paid for school lunches and over half of whom lived with both parents.

A range of quantitative measures were used and the findings show that Black students were seriously under-represented in gifted programmes and were also under-identified as gifted. In fact, when school districts were initially contacted to identify gifted Black pupils only 42 (28%) were suggested. As a consequence, Ford consulted both school records for Grade Point Average (GPA) and achievement test scores and created a further category including pupils with high potential.

Ford's study found no evidence to suggest a correlation between achievement level and racial identity. Students held positive attitudes towards curriculum subjects and school in general, as well as having positive attitudes towards gifted students and gifted programmes. She did, however, observe differences between achievement attitudes and achievement behaviours. Students tended not to express concern about pressure.

Studies which focus on Black achievers have received little attention in the British literature and, as a result, valuable insights have been lost. Research in this area needs to question, for example: How do such pupils achieve? What factors contribute to their success? How many of these factors are attributable to the pupil, school or family? Are some schools more successful than others? To what extent do school ethos, classroom climate, teacher-pupil interaction and relationships, home-school links and attitudes of pupils and teachers contribute to the achievement levels of Black pupils? The research on positive classrooms and gifted Black students is clearly worthy of further exploration and warrants an extended treatment of its own.

Conclusion

This chapter has attempted to outline the nature and extent of under-performance of Black children. Recent research within the interpretive tradition offers many promising new lines of inquiry. Researchers have begun to consider underperformance from a Black perspective, and have attempted to describe the characteristics of positive classrooms, high achieving Black students and successful teachers of Black students. This last vein of research offers alternative ways forward which will be pursued in greater depth later in this book.

Chapter 3

Language and the curriculum

The language used by the Black community in the UK, USA and the Caribbean has been identified as one of the factors contributing to the poor performance of Black children in the educational system. Additionally, research has shown that teacher perspectives towards Black language can influence teacher-pupil interaction and may thus affect the educational outcomes of the Black child.

This chapter traces attitudes towards Caribbean heritage languages. It then goes on to consider educational responses to language diversity. Finally, it points towards the potential critical language awareness approaches in providing rich learning environments which not only educate but also liberate and empower pupils in British schools.

Caribbean heritage varieties in Britain

The current linguistic situation of Caribbean heritage children in Britain is interesting from both a sociolinguistic and an educational perspective. The variety spoken by many Black youths has variously been described as Black British English (Sutcliffe, 1982), Patois (Edwards, 1986), British Jamaican Creole (Sutcliffe, 1992) and London Jamaican (Rosen and Burgess, 1980; Hewitt, 1986; Sebba, 1986, 1993). This range of labels illustrates both the complexity and the variation found in Black British speech. Sutcliffe (1982:157), for example, in his study of Caribbean born and Black British youth in Bedford observes that:

Behind this variation lies a complicated value system in which English is not just a 'formal' language, or a necessary mainstream accomplishment for participation in the wider society, or even as a means of communicating in full with White classmates and playmates. It is also part of the Caribbean culture that these children have inherited and are re-creating to suit their own particular needs in Britain.

Several studies have been conducted in order to describe the language varieties spoken by the Black community in Britain. Viv Edwards (1976, 1979) for instance, reports on the presence of West Indian varieties in British schools and examines the effect of linguistic differences on children's understanding of standard English texts. She also reports research on attitudes towards West Indian language: teacher groups, as well as pupils, Black and White, showed a hierarchy of preferences with standard English speakers considered most competent and intelligent, followed by working class White children and, finally, West Indian children.

Sutcliffe (1982) considers a range of issues which are pertinent to the Black British community. As part of his study, he elicits the responses on language use of forty seven first and second generation Caribbean origin children living in Bedford. He notes that creole use was especially marked in friend to friend conversation, sibling to sibling talk, and parent to child discourse. It was less pronounced, however, in child to parent interaction.

The first major sociolinguistic investigation to be undertaken into the language of the Black community in Britain is reported in Edwards (1986). Her study is based on the language behaviour of forty five young people of Jamaican heritage living in Dudley, West Midlands. She examines the relationship of three scores – Patois frequency, Patois competence and patterns of Patois usage – with various explanatory variables including social network, education, gender and attitudes to mainstream society.

Although not directly concerned with the language of the Black community, Hewitt's (1988) observations of interracial friendship among adolescents highlight the use of Creole as a marker of friendship and solidarity.

Sutcliffe's (1992) study is based on the same data as Edwards (1986). He posits the view that grammatical elements of African languages have been retained in the diaspora. He points, for instance, to similarities which exist among West African Kwa languages, Black English in the USA and British Jamaican Creole.

Sebba's (1993) study is based on conversational data recorded by young Black British people in south London. An unspecified number of respondents from a range of Caribbean island origins took part in the study. The data collection is divided into two parts. Initially informants were left alone in pairs and asked to 'talk Black' or 'chat Patois'. Later, some informants took recording equipment into their homes and recorded conversations between their families and friends.

Two important issues central to discussion of the language used by the Black community in Britain today emerge from the studies cited above: the relationship between language choice and identity and the range of language varieties available to Black British speakers. These concerns are considered below.

Language and identity

Language is a powerful symbol of cultural identity and several commentators have reported that the language choices of young Black people are closely linked to their identification with the Black community. Edwards (1986), for instance, demonstrates that the more strongly young people identify with Black culture, the greater the frequency of Patois features in their speech, the greater their competence in Patois and the wider the range of situations in which they use Patois features.

Various other writers make similar observations. Bones (1986), for example, notes that in Jamaica Rastafarians regard Patois as the language of Africans and feel a strong sense of commitment towards its maintenance and development. Dalphinis (1991:49), reporting on the use of Patois in Britain, observes that:

> The use of Patois for British Blacks can thus be seen very clearly as an identity issue. The choice of distinctively Black features in young people's speech is a positive assertion of their Black identity and a rejection of the low status accorded to Black people and their speech in mainstream White society.

Many scholars (cf. Hewitt, 1986; Edwards, 1986) have pointed to the use of Patois not only as a marker of identity but also as an expression of resistance to the dominant culture. Wong (1986: 113), writing on the use of Creole as a language of power and solidarity, claims that language represents

> ... an edifice on which is constructed racial pride and power as well as a defence against the assimilationist encroachment of the dominant society.

More recently Brandt (1990) asserts that African-Caribbean youth are using Creole as part of symbolic resistance to standard English. In sum, for many young Black people in Britain, language choice not only reflects identity with Black culture, but also, a reaction to the dominant society and its language.

One variety or more?

Edwards (1986) argues that whereas Creole use in the Caribbean occurs along a continuum ranging from the standard (acrolect) to broad patois (basilect), with several intermediate varieties (mesolects), the situation of Black British speakers is quite different. These speakers, she asserts, are more inclined to 'prefer polar variants and to avoid the intermediate forms' (p.51). Sutcliffe (1992:1) also points to the use of two codes. He argues that:

> British Black Jamaican (BJC) is used bilingually with standard or regional English: London English or 'Cockney' in the London area, Black Country English in the West Midlands conurbation, and so on, as a reflection of the experience of being 'Black in a White world'.

Later, he reports that the situation of Caribbean heritage children...

> is very clear... many young speakers, perhaps 30% of the total population of the Black community, or more, have been involved in a very obvious language shift, from the Eastern and Southern Caribbean varieties of their parents, to a new, solidary variety of urban Jamaican Creole (p. 106).

Writing on a similar theme, Sebba (1993) reports that, whilst it is usual in the case of a language which has formed in a contact situation to go through a process of 'levelling' and 'simplification', this is not the case for Caribbean creoles in London. He asserts that Caribbean heritage children born in Britain use two codes. He also highlights geographical differences which, by and large, are influenced by local varieties of British English. He concludes that Black British children do not necessarily have to be of Jamaican descent to speak Jamaican Creole:

> Young Black Londoners do not speak a 'British Caribbean Creole' with features drawn from many Caribbean varieties. Rather, they acknowledge two distinct and separable codes. When they are not speaking London English, they may choose to 'talk Black' or 'chat Patois': but this 'Black' variety is focussed on Jamaican Creole in particular (p. 43).

It has been reported, for instance, that Dominican heritage speakers living in Bradford use a variety that bears all the hallmarks of Jamaican creole (Tate, 1984; Sebba and Tate, 1986). Similar observations have been made about the language of London school children (Rosen and Burgess, 1980; Hewitt, 1986).

Whilst it is indisputable that many Caribbean heritage children use Black variants as part of their speech repertoire, the extent to which these varieties are influenced by Jamaican creole is debatable. The assumption that all Caribbean heritage children regardless of island of parental origin speak a Jamaican influenced variety is certainly open to question.

It is speculative to suggest that the Black variety is always of Jamaican origin. My observations indicate that many Caribbean heritage children not only use a variety which is focused on aspects of Jamaican Creole, but also that children whose heritage is not Jamaican have access to and varying levels of competence in the Creole of their forebears. My own patterns of code-switching are a case in point. For example, when 'talking Black' amongst friends or intimates, the variety I invariably select is Bajan. I do, however, also have access to a variety which is influenced by Jamaican Creole. The selection of one variant as opposed to the other is dependent on a number of factors, such as the topic under discussion, the age and origins of the other speakers and the social context. I am not unique in this respect: I have observed this same phenomenon amongst many other speakers. Choice of Black variety, then, may reflect the affinity one feels towards the other participants or it may represent a positive assertion of an individual's island origin. In the absence of a regional survey of the language behaviour of Caribbean heritage young people in Britain, the influence of Jamaican Creole remains unclear. As Edwards (1986: 134) points out:

It is also interesting to speculate what the situation would be in High Wycombe where the majority Black population comes from St. Vincent, or in Slough where there are large numbers of Anguillans.

To this one could add the Barbadians in Reading and the Kittians in Leeds. Moreover, the speech of first generation Black British is likely to differ significantly from the language behaviour of the second and third generation. New words and features are constantly evolving. For instance, whilst first generation might recognise the term 'banachek' to refer to a person who regularly socialises with White people, the second and third generation now use terms such as 'bounty' and 'coconut'.

Attitudes to Black varieties

Black language is regular and rule-governed and is the vehicle for a lively and varied oral culture. Unfortunately it is still, in many areas, regarded as an inferior and 'bastardised' derivative of standard English. Throughout the centuries negative attitudes towards Black language have prevailed. In a preface to *Black Border* (1922), Ambrose Gonzales, for instance, wrote of the Gullah dialect spoken by the Black population on the islands off the coast of South Carolina, USA:

> The [Gullah] words are, of course, not African, for the African brought over or retained only a few words of his jungle tongue, and even these few are by no means authenticated as part of the original scant baggage of the negro slaves... Slovenly and careless of speech, these Gullahs seized upon the peasant English used by some of the early settlers and by the White servants of the wealthier Colonists, wrapped their clumsy tongues about it as well they could, and, enriched with certain expressive African words, it issued through their flat noses and thick lips so workable a form of speech that it was gradually adopted by the other slaves and became in time the accepted Negro speech of the lower districts of South Carolina and Georgia. With characteristic laziness, these Gullah negroes took short cuts to the ears of their auditors using as few words as possible, sometimes making one gender serve for three, one tense for several, and totally disregarding singular and plural numbers (cited in Smitherman, 1977:172).

Two main assumptions emerge from this description. Firstly, it is suggested that Black language represents an approximation to the language of White slavers. However, as the discussion above shows, creoles are languages in their own right which have evolved in a situation of multilingual contact. As in any situation where speakers of different varieties come together, the new language inevitably draws on features of the dominant as well the subordinate languages. Further, there is no doubt that creoles are regular and rule-governed languages.

Secondly, the description points to the supposed inferiority of the language and its speakers, a position which has been strongly refuted by sociolinguistic research. J. Edwards (1979:138) for example, claims that:

> Language and language varieties are all valid symbolic systems; distinctions among them cannot be justifiably attributed to greater or lesser logical force, accuracy, etc.

It is a social fact that some varieties are considered to be superior, more eloquent and logical than others. Hudson (1983:195), for instance, refers to the social stereotyping of speech as 'linguistic prejudice' and notes that speech is frequently used to locate a 'speaker's social characteristics'. In sum, our attitudes towards language are conditioned by our social, political and regional biases.

Evidence for this position comes from Lambert, Hodgson and Fillenbaum (1960). Using the matched guise technique, (where judges evaluate samples of speech from the same speaker while assuming that they are from different speakers) French and English speaking college students in Montreal evaluated speakers' personalities after hearing them read passages in English and French. After listening to samples of speech, the students were asked to assess the speakers along a range of dimensions which included ambition, intelligence and sense of humour. Lambert *et al* report that the English judges rated English speakers more highly on most dimensions. The French judges, however, not only judged the English guises more favourably than the French ones but they also judged French speakers less favourably than did the English judges. In short, majority and minority group speakers recognise majority group speakers as more intelligent, competent etc. However, minority group speakers consider other minority speakers more sincere and trustworthy.

Although this phenomenon was first demonstrated with French and English Canadians it has since been noted in other minority groups (see for instance, studies undertaken in Jewish, French Canadian and Black communities such as Lambert, 1967; Tucker and Lambert, 1969; Carranza and Ryan, 1975 and Irwin, 1977).

Giles, Bourhis, Trudgill and Lewis (1974) claim that there are two possible hypotheses to explain this phenomenon. The 'inherent value' hypothesis asserts that certain accents possess intrinsic qualities that make them more pleasing to the ear. The 'imposed norm' hypothesis, in contrast, holds that the high status accorded to particular accents and their 'accepted pleasantness' are merely reflections of the status of their speakers. In order to verify their claims, they played recordings of different language varieties to judges who were unfamiliar with the varieties or their status implications. The findings revealed that listeners did not show any pattern of preferences for the different language varieties. Thus the 'inherent value' hypothesis did not hold. The validation of the 'imposed norm' hypothesis underlines the powerful nature of the social stereotyping of speech.

Attitudes towards Caribbean varieties in schools

The debate surrounding Black language and education from the 1960s onwards provides many examples of negative attitudes towards Caribbean varieties. For instance, a report by the National Association of School Masters describes Caribbean languages as a 'kind of plantation English which is socially unacceptable and inadequate for communication' (cited in Edwards, 1986: 25). Similar conclusions about the nature of Caribbean language were drawn by the Birmingham branch of the Association of Teachers of English to Pupils from Overseas (ATEPO) who assert that Caribbean language is 'babyish, careless and slovenly, lacking proper grammar and very relaxed like the way they walk'. Writing in 1977, Max Morris, a London headteacher, vehemently rejects the notion of placing creoles on the curriculum:

> Should I put creole on my time-table? Over my dead body and the majority of my parents would cheer me to the skies. They want their children to get jobs (cited in Edwards, 1979:109).

Such attitudes are not confined to White observers. Members of the Black community also express negative views towards their language, which is frequently referred to as 'bad' or 'broken' English. Dodd (1993) writing in an article on the low pass rate of Jamaican children in the English language Caribbean Examinations Council (CXC) exam, expresses the following view perpetuating popular prejudice:

> Patois is not an African language which is preserved as Catalans preserved their language in Spain. Patois is a bastard, made up of mis-pronounced English words, pieces of Akan dialect, as well as others, mixed into a mush by usage.

Negative attitudes towards Caribbean people and their languages have served to exacerbate issues surrounding Black language and attainment in British schools. Moreover, the attitudes of sections of the Black community have led to further confusion about the intrinsic value of Creole.

Language has often been regarded as central to debates on educational achievement. In the case of children of Caribbean heritage, these debates influenced official responses to the presence of Caribbean varieties in British schools. Many writers, for instance, have pointed to the relationship between the poor performance of Black children and their perceived language difficulties, and it is to a discussion of these concerns that we now turn.

The National Curriculum

It has been suggested that a statutory National Curriculum for all children in Britain will lead to the marginalisation of minority languages and cultures. The 1988 Education Reform Act (ERA) signalled the most dramatic change in British education policy since 1944. A national curriculum was introduced comprising three core subjects (English, Maths and Science) and six foundation subjects (Art, History, Geography, Technology, Music and Physical Education). All pupils in the state sector would be assessed at four key stages at the ages of 7, 11, 14 and 16.

There had been mounting concern that standards in spoken and written English were in decline. The Conservative government was keen to halt not only what it saw as the deteriorating standards of English but also the growing weaknesses of society in general. In a Radio Four interview, Norman Tebbit, a senior cabinet minister typifies this approach to education:

We've allowed so many standards to slip... teachers weren't bothering to teach kids to spell and to punctuate properly... If you allow standards to slip to the stage where good English is no better than bad English, where people turn up filthy ... at school ... All those things tend to cause people to have no standards at all, once you lose standards then there's no imperative to stay out of crime (quoted in Graddol and Swann, 1988:102).

Thus English was placed firmly on the political agenda and positioned along with the moral decline of society and the increase in crime. The general preoccupation with 'order' continued during the 1980s and other public figures expressed similar views. For instance, Prince Charles declared that:

We've got to produce people who can write proper English. It's a fundamental problem... If we want people who can write good English and write plays for the future, it cannot be done with the present system, and all the nonsense academics come up with. It's a fundamental problem. We must educate for character. That's the trouble with schools. They don't educate for character. This matters a great deal. The whole way schools are operating is not right. I do not believe English is being taught properly. You cannot educate people properly unless you do it on a basic frame-work and drilling system (Business in the Community conference, County Hall, London: 28th June, 1989).

In order to develop a national framework for English teaching in the UK, the government commissioned an inquiry (the Kingman Inquiry), whose aims were to recommend a 'model' of the English language, knowledge of which would form one aspect of the English curriculum, while also informing initial teacher training programmes. The final Report (DES, 1988), however, rejected a return to traditional grammar, suggesting instead that children should acquire 'knowledge about language'.

Whilst recognising the validity of English dialects, the Kingman Report acknowledged the importance of acquiring standard English:

The dialect usages of family and immediate circle are sufficient to their purposes; but membership of the smaller group entails membership of the larger, and for the wider community – that of the nation and the world – the standard language will be indispensable. Of course, in acquiring the standard language, we do not abandon the variation – each has its own authenticity, and to move with facility between them is to develop a versatility in language, a linguistic repertoire, which should be open to all (p. 7).

If we look more closely at the underlying assumptions made in this statement and in the Kingman Report generally, it becomes apparent that non-standard varieties are, in effect, given little status and are relegated to informal domains, while Standard British English is 'indispensable'. Later in the document, the status of standard English is made more explicit:

> It is possible that a generation of our children may grow up deprived of their entitlement – an introduction to the powerful and splendid history of the best that has been thought and said in our language (p. 11).

An important question here, nonetheless, is whose language does the report refer to? References to the 'nation' imply a single British identity, a description which fails to acknowledge the multicultural and multilingual nature of British society.

Cameron and Bourne (1988:147), writing on the symbolic position of grammar in the Kingman Report, observe its position as 'a key ideological text about the state of the English language and its relation to the state of the Nation'. Further, they assert that governmental response to the teaching of English is inextricably linked to issues of national identity and culture. Whereas grammar is a neutral term for linguists, for non-specialists it is bound up with concepts such as tradition, authority, hierarchy, order and rules. So:

> Attitudes to grammar are concerned with attitudes to authority; anxieties about grammar are at some deeper level anxieties about the breakdown of order and tradition, not just in language but in society at large (p. 150).

Authoritarian states, they argue, promote the idea of national language as a way of promoting feelings of solidarity and oneness. As a consequence, the notion of linguistic diversity becomes threatening and represents a challenge that should be contained or eliminated. Kingman's recommendations regarding standard English and its failure to acknowledge the linguistic diversity existing in Britain both have the effect of marginalising minority varieties. There is no mention, for instance, of the effects of race or class on language. Rather, variation is discussed in terms of its historical and geographical significance. Such an approach clearly does not take into account the language needs of minority groups. In fact, there is very little of direct concern to bi/multilingual and bidilectical pupils. Cameron and Bourne claim that:

> The covert function of the model is to strengthen and protect English at the expense of other languages; and this becomes overt in the Secretary of State's notes of 'Supplementary Guidance' to the national curriculum working group on English which took over where Kingman left off. The notes enjoin readers to bear in mind 'the cardinal point that English should be the first language and medium of instruction for all pupils in England' (p. 153).

The full effects of the imposition of a Eurocentric curriculum upon non-standard and bilingual speakers remain to be seen. There is evidence, however, to suggest that, in implementing the National Curriculum English Orders, some teachers are behaving in ways that marginalise non-standard speakers and reinforce stereotypical notions of status (cf. Aldwin, 1996).

Steele (1993), for example, reports a situation where the words of a traditional Jamaican song 'Come back Liza' were changed to standard English by a teacher at a school attended by her friend's daughter. The words, 'Everytime I think pon Liza, water come a mi eye' were substituted with standard English, 'tears come to my eyes'. Whilst it may be argued that this teacher may be misguided and acting insensitively, this situation raises some important issues for current practice. For instance, how, what and when does a teacher correct what they perceive as incorrect without marginalising non-standard and bilingual speakers? The National Curriculum English Orders clearly acknowledge the important links between language and identity and highlight the damaging effects that indiscriminate 'corrections' can have on motivation and self-esteem. One implication of the recent legislation is becoming clear. As Steele (1993: 14) asserts:

> Children will no longer be actively encouraged to develop into confident and competent communicators who are articulate in their use of a range of language registers, including Standard English. They will, instead, be required, by law, to adapt their spoken language to the conventions of Standard English.

Language awareness

Verbatim interpretation of the English National Curriculum document clearly limits the potential of a language education which builds on children's existing knowledge of their own language use and of that used by those around them. Advocates of language awareness and critical language awareness, however, have indicated ways in which 'knowledge about language' can be used not only to educate but also to liberate those groups in society who have traditionally been in low status positions.

Language awareness encourages children to explore language use and attitudes. It has developed rapidly in British schools and is now sometimes promoted as an area of study in its own right. Such activities can be extremely useful to inform children of the varieties present in the Caribbean – but there are difficulties. Patois has not been regarded in the same way as community languages such as Urdu and Gujerati and some commentators have argued strongly against its inclusion in the curriculum. They have claimed, for example, that such activities are inappropriate and counterproductive. Stone (1981: 112) argues that the school should aim to ensure familiarity and competence in the standard and let the home and the family be responsible for the maintenance of the dialect:

> Without saying that dialect should never be formally used in schools, I would argue that it is the job of the school to enable children to function with ease in the standard language. By the same token it is the job of the home, family and community to keep the dialect alive.

She goes on to suggest that the introduction of Patois into the curriculum serves to uphold the legitimate culture of the school against the 'heretical' culture of Black people and observes that the legitimisation of Patois will lead to the formation of new varieties that will simply replace the present ones. Carby (1980) adds weight to this view, observing that teacher knowledge of dialect cannot eradicate racism in schools or in the larger society.

These observations, however, apply to traditional language awareness activities and it has been suggested that the ability of language awareness to challenge the status quo has been seriously underestimated (Clark, Fairclough, Ivanic and Jones, 1991). There is no reason why discussions about language cannot take on a more critical stance. There is, they argue, scope to discuss issues pertaining to linguistic inequality, racism, sexism and the social origins and status of standard English.

Critical language awareness describes the discourse of a society *and* offers explanations of it. As a social practice language pervades all spheres of life. Thus much language behaviour is largely unconscious and many established language practices consequently remain unchallenged. They assert that although language is determined by 'conventions', it is socially determined and therefore allows its users the facility to critique those same conventions. Clark *et al* conclude that language acts as practice and a site of struggle. Moreover, critical language awareness can assist in the development of consciousness and self-consciousness among dominated people.

Corson (1993) proposes three ways in which critical language awareness may be implemented in schools. Firstly, children should be encouraged to look at meanings more critically and not take them for granted. Secondly, students can investigate the reasons why some varieties of language are given lesser status than others. Lastly, pupils can be helped not only to challenge the status quo but also to effect change. Teachers also play an important part. By encouraging children critically to examine the discourse practices of the school, a model is established. This may be used within the school and more widely in the world outside school. Corson concludes that

> If mundane discourse practices in schools are not tied in children's minds to a critical awareness of that discourse set in its wider context, then the discourse conceals the structures of domination within which it is located. In doing so, it creates a deceitful illusion of freedom which is clearly miseducative (p. 207).

Language awareness and critical language awareness, then, provide new insights to the study of language which are particularly useful to minority and majority students. There is a need, nonetheless, to ensure that verbatim interpretation of the English document does not impede teachers' ability to investigate language issues nor deprive children of their right to an informed and holistic education.

Conclusion

In this chapter we have considered the linguistic situation of children of Caribbean heritage in Britain and have noted the way that the language varieties used are influenced by a number of factors including social network and identity. Further, writers have pointed towards the emergence of a stable Jamaican influenced variety. This is an area, however, where much work needs to be done. Although many Caribbean heritage children may well use a variety focused on Jamaican Creole, the fact that they may be influenced by other creoles requires further investigation.

Black language varieties have been, and are still, subject to negative evaluations. Such views have been perpetuated not only by teachers but also by members of the Black community. Moreover, it has been argued that recent changes in educational policy, which are underpinned by notions of a single nation and oneness, will have the effect of marginalising minority languages and their speakers.

Proponents of critical language awareness, however, assert that it is possible for schools to challenge established language practices. By developing a greater awareness and a critical attitude, children can focus on the reasons why some varieties are thought better than others.

Chapter 4

Language, culture and the schooling process

A feature of contemporary debate into the underperformance of Black children in the diaspora has been the role of culture in the process of schooling. Where such discussions have taken place they have centred on perceived cultural characteristics of Black children which militate against success in school. Consequently, it has been reported on both sides of the Atlantic that aspects of Black culture are misinterpreted by majority teachers – with potentially damaging effects for Black students, especially boys.

This chapter focuses in more detail on the way in which differences in culture manifest themselves in the educational arena. The work of Bourdieu is explored as a means of providing a framework within which to look at questions of language, culture and schooling as they relate to Black pupils. The discussion then moves to a consideration of British and American research in this area. African-American and African Caribbean culture is examined and the differing responses to these groups of pupils are observed. Finally, we look at new areas of investigation on the causes of underperformance in Black children, drawing on pertinent work in the USA and the UK, and a small number of personal accounts by Black teachers. The chapter concludes by highlighting the role of Black educators in multi-ethnic schools, pointing to their dual relationship with the Black community and the educational establishment.

The role of schooling as a form of social and cultural reproduction

French social theorist Pierre Bourdieu presents a convincing line of argument which illustrates how factors within societies and cultures preserve and recreate traditions and conventions within those same societies and cultures. Language, an intrinsic part of interpersonal communication, is a key element in this process and is therefore embedded within social reproduction. Each individual is both teacher and learner, since in the process of learning everyday acts we are invariably providing or learning from models.

Bourdieu's notion of 'habitus' – a system of enduring characteristics – is, he argues, at the core of an individual's behaviour. The habitus held in common by the dominant group permeates schooling, yet habitus can only be obtained via family upbringing. Schools, Bourdieu asserts, do not state their position explicitly but it is grounded in definitions of success. Groups who hold alternative habitus have little purchase on the culture of schooling. It is important to point out that Bourdieu does not allude to some form of linguistic deficit amongst social groups, rather, he argues that the language of social groups; is comprised of many different types of relations, which are, in turn, rooted in different dispositions and attitudes towards the material world and other people.

Traditions and conventions, including codes of language, thus become re-invented and remoulded, even though larger patterns of culture and language appear undifferentiated. Part of this process of reproduction means that some behavioural traditions achieve special status, thus giving its possessors status. Such respected conventions are passed on to others, especially offspring who benefit from the social advantages that are passed with them.

Bourdieu presents the relations between language and culture as a series of metaphors. Culture is seen an economic system, and 'cultural capital' as those culturally esteemed advantages which people acquire as part of their life experiences, peer groups and family backgrounds. 'Academic capital' is inherited as it is the guaranteed by-product of cultural transmission which occurs through the home and school. He also speaks of 'linguistic capital'- the most important part of cultural heritage.

Linguistic capital includes more than just the ability to produce well-formed grammatical expressions; it also incorporates the ability to utilise appropriate norms for language use and to produce the correct expressions for the right 'linguistic markets'. Using Bourdieu's analyses it is fair to suggest that there are many linguistic markets which yield profit for the user, and where non-standard or low status languages are assigned limited value. Therefore, children in those markets remain silent in school or withdraw from them (a point discussed in more detail later in this chapter).

Commenting on the cultural or linguistic capital that is valued in schools, Bourdieu observes that schools operate on the basis that all children have equal access to schooling. By rewarding pupils with qualifications and the like (high status capital), schools actively reproduce a situation that is favourable to some. This process of symbolic power, then, reproduces unequal educational outcomes for minority group children, including Black children.

Education systems and culture

In Britain there has not been a tradition of discussion which focuses on culture and the schooling experiences of African Caribbean pupils and whilst the social, historical and economic circumstances surrounding the African-American community in the USA differ in many respects to that of the African Caribbean community in Britain, they do nonetheless share similar features in terms of the learning outcomes of Black children.

The work of Wade Boykin has been particularly influential in this debate. Writing on the schooling of Black children in the USA, Boykin (1994) observes that matters pertaining to culture are gaining increased currency in contemporary educational debate. He points also to the tendency for these debates to exclude matters of culture 'which reside in the very marrow of the schooling process' (p. 123). Boykin argues that in order fully to understand the position of culture in education, it is necessary to do so at the level of deep structure, and this entails acknowledging that cultural phenomena undergird the foundations on which education is based.

The presence of cultural forms of reference within education inevitably means that some children enter school with greater levels of preparedness – either knowing what the cultural rules are, or being in a position to accept them more readily. Others may not be so well prepared and are likely to be penalised for not knowing the cultural rules or for appearing resistant to the culture of power in schools.

But how does this culture of power manifest itself? By and large these cultural rules remain unconscious, but in the United States it has been possible to identify key areas which remain static and form part of the expected, and accepted, norms of school life. In answering this question several commentators have highlighted the significance of specific features including, for instance, impulse control where there is an emphasis on reason over emotion and a tendency to expend effort in tasks which are unrelated to personal wants, goals or motives (Krate, 1975). Gay (1975) has also contributed to the discussion, observing that schools show preferences for movement restriction and focus on task rather than people orientation. Others have pointed to delayed gratification, adherence to clock time (where time is perceived as a commodity) and to links between individual status and possessions (Katz, 1975), as components of the school culture.

Boykin argues that factors such as these are at the very root of education as they have been conceived and practiced in the United States. They form part of the accoutrements associated with education, influencing teacher expectations and ultimately pedagogic practices. He argues that when children are socialised into the routines of schooling such as providing individual work with individualised answers; when they perceive that moving out of their seats is inappropriate; when they confine their learning to allocated slots of time, then they 'are pervasively having cultural lessons imposed on them' (p. 125).

Boykin concedes that children need to master the range of tasks that teachers require of them but argues that 'when factors like emotional containment and delay of gratification are seen not as culturally valued expressions but, rather, as signs of 'social maturity'... and when children are penalised for not knowing that such elements are part of the behavioural rules (or because they display alternative expressions), such children are 'put at a needless disadvantage' (p. 126).

In response to the cultural gaps that exist in traditional American educational practices and its failure to provide culturally congruent learning contexts for African-American children, Boykin contests that systematic efforts to incorporate what he calls an 'Afro-Cultural Ethos' are needed. This ethos is manifested in the daily lives of African-Americans and is firmly grounded in West African retentions which prevail throughout the diaspora.

The elements which comprise African-cultural ethos include: *spirituality* – where life is seen as vitalistic rather than mechanistic; *harmony* – human existence and nature viewing as surviving interdependently and in harmony; *movement* – where there is an emphasis on rhythm, music and dance; verve – a tendency for high levels of stimulation; *affect* – an emphasis on emotion and feelings; *communalism* – a commitment to social connectedness and an aware-ness that group responsibility pervades individual privilege; *expressive individualism* – placing value on genuine personal expression; *oral tradition* – a preference for oral/aural communication which values language that utilises metaphors, alliteration and colourful forms; and *social time perspective* – an orientation which views time as social rather than material space.

By incorporating an African-cultural ethos, Boykin argues, Black cultural capital is increased and so there is greater 'intersubjectivity' – that is, increased mutual understanding, or an understanding of each other's understanding (Gergen, 1980). Or, in Boykin's succinct phrase, being 'on the same cultural page' is essential to successful inter-subjectivity. He observes that three separate but related pedagogical concerns need to be addressed in the analysis of cultural deep structure.

First is Afro-cultural integrity. At present, American schools do not demonstrate regard for the Afro-cultural experience and this may have implications for teacher attitude and expectations. For instance, Afro-cultural displays are likely to viewed in negative terms and teacher expectations may not be positive. Ultimately, situations such as these can lead to oppositional stances and create contests of power in the classroom.

Secondly, Boykin notes that where no effort is made to incorporate Afro-cultural continuity, that is, existing conceptual competencies that have developed outside of formal schooling it can affect motivational levels. Furthermore, students may refuse to take part in certain activities because they perceive that they violate cultural norms. On the other hand, where continuity is expressed it is likely that existing and emerging skills will be displayed and adopted in formal school settings. In addition, greater opportunities for academic task development provides a platform where 'school can become, perhaps, an outlet for the positive, proactive, and constructive renditions of Afro-cultural expression' (p.129).

Thirdly, mainstream cultural fluency which resides at the heart of American education is likely to remain firmly on the school agenda. Boykin asserts that children can become more fluent in the overriding school agenda, but notes that this does not equate with the internalisation of mainstream culture *per se*. Rather, the mainstream socialisation function should be taught explicitly and should not devalue any existing cultural frames of reference. He goes on to argue that teachers should focus on maximising instances where an Afro-cultural factor can facilitate the learning process, but notes that they should also know when it is inappropriate. Black children, he states, 'should learn to become discriminating in their use of their cultural capital ... that is, they must learn to discern the time and place for use of certain expressions and that every academic instance will not an be occasion for expression of the Afro-cultural ethos' (p. 134).

Writing in a similar vein, Irvine (1990) refers to what is termed 'cultural synchronisation', which she bases on anthropological and historical research. Cultural synchronisation advances the theory that African-Americans have a distinct culture which is rooted in identifiable norms, language, behaviours and attitudes from West Africa. She observes three cultural characteristics which are problematic for African-American children in predominantly White middle-class school settings: style (or manner of personal presentation); use of Black English; and cognition or processes of knowing and perceiving.

Questions of 'style' in the classroom

Unlike their White peers, then, Black children experience a disproportionate amount of negative interaction in the classroom. The arrival in Britain of large numbers of Caribbean immigrants during the late 1950s and early 1960s signalled a new era of British history. Many people left the Caribbean with dreams of starting a new life in the 'mother country' which would eventually lead to a higher standard of living and improved life chances for their children. Once they arrived, however, far from being welcome, they were subjected to overt racism, particularly concerning housing, employment and education (Husband, 1982). Three and a half decades later, there is a new generation of Black British children and Black teachers in the school system. Yet Black achievement remains poor compared to that of the indigenous population (DES, 1985; Kysel, 1988; Mirza, 1992) and Black teachers are often found in the lower echelons of the teaching profession (Hubah 1984; Brar, 1991).

Research in British schools (see, for instance, Wright, 1986, 1992; Gillborn, 1988, 1990a, 1990b; Mac an Ghaill, 1988; Ogilvy et al, 1992; Troyna, 1991) has drawn attention to the daily experiences of non-White children in British schools These studies indicate that White teachers' expectations, perceptions and opinions of minority pupils can, and do, affect the quality and frequency of interactions with such pupils. As a result these students experience a disproportionate amount of conflict and criticism which may seriously affect their eventual educational outcomes.

The majority of these negative interactions are enacted primarily over language. This is not to suggest that other factors do not play an important part. In the context of the current discussion, however, the study of language provides a useful starting-point for an assessment of the ways in which inequalities are perpetuated through education, one of the most important channels of socialisation.

Ways of being in the Black community

Black verbal culture – the style of speaking which has evolved in Africa, America and the Caribbean – has been studied in a variety of contexts. Black language has been the subject of many investigations, relating not only to the forms of words used but also the social and situational contexts in which it occurs (Mitchell-Kernan, 1972; Abrahams, 1976; Sutcliffe, 1982; Edwards, 1986; Hewitt, 1986).

Attention has also been paid to the differences between Black and White rhetorical modes. Kochman (1981:97) for instance, observes two distinct speech behaviours when Blacks and Whites engage in public debate. Blacks, he suggests, adopt a mode of behaviour which is 'high-keyed, animated, interpersonal and confrontational', whereas Whites are 'low-keyed, dispassionate, impersonal and non-challenging'. The conversational rules of turn-taking observed among White speakers are not strictly adhered to in the Black speech event, and there is a tendency to interrupt when you can – speakers who assert themselves and keep up with the flow of the talk are assigned greater value than those who do not. Kochman also reports that, due to the competitive nature of Black discourse, it is not unusual for two people to speak at the same time, although they may not necessarily be addressing the same audience. Reisman (1974) makes similar observations, talking, for instance, of the 'contrapuntal' nature of Black discourse.

Smitherman (1977:16) pursues a similar theme, and makes an interesting distinction between 'language' and 'style'. The term 'language', she argues, refers to 'sounds and grammatical structures' whereas 'style' describes the ways in which speakers convey meaning in a larger context. In short, 'language is words and style is what you do with words'.

Writing on the oral traditions of Jamaican society, Martha Warren Beckwith (1929), cited in Sutcliffe and Tomlin, 1986) observed that Jamaicans actualise their 'inner life' through sound and motion. The striking differences that are found between Black and White verbal and non-verbal discourse styles can give rise to difficulties for the non-White child living in a predominantly White society. Two important questions arise: firstly, whether Black children experience a cultural clash of verbal and non-verbal styles and, secondly, is there a real possibility that Black children's energy levels are in direct conflict with the authority structure of schools?

Recent research does, in fact, indicate that Black children may face difficulties in obtaining 'a good education' because they display certain cultural characteristics which some teachers interpret as anti-authoritarian and rebellious (Gillborn, 1990a). Studies of the Black community have suggested that 'style' has an important influence on Black language. Kochman (1981:130) defines style as:

> an attitude that individuals within a culture express through their choice of cultural form... Black style is more self-conscious, more expressive, more expansive, more colourful, more intense, more assertive, more aggressive, and more focused on the individual than is the style of the larger society of which Blacks are part.

Kochman further asserts that style permeates every aspect of life, including language, body language and dress. In the field of education, however, there is growing evidence that one aspect of style, the body language of Black children, is being interpreted by some teachers as expressing insolence and reluctance to conform to classroom rules. It has also been linked to the disproportionate numbers of African-Caribbean children being excluded from school, particularly Black boys.

Local Education Authorities too, are now attaching importance to this question. For instance, a study of Birmingham Local Education Authority (LEA) conducted by the Commission for Racial Equality (CRE) in 1985 reported that Black children represented nine per cent of its total school population of 216,344, yet accounted for 40 per cent of suspensions. Their UK White and Irish peers, in contrast, represented 42 per cent of the school population, but only 13 per cent of suspensions. The report states that 'both the records relating to suspensions and the accounts of witnesses suggest that difficulties arise when teachers misinterpret Black pupils' behaviour. This can lead to over-reaction by pupil and teacher alike' (p.48). An example of one such misunderstanding is the way some Black pupils lower their eyes when confronted by a teacher – a mark of respect in the Caribbean community was being interpreted as a sign of 'insolence' in school.

In similar vein, a report on Nottingham secondary schools observed that Black children's body language often leads teachers to think that they were 'arrogant, insolent, defiant, aggressive, disruptive and looking for trouble'. Examples given by the teachers included 'the way Afro-Caribbean pupils look at them, walk in an arrogant, exaggerated way, display dumb insolence, look away when challenged, and suck and hiss their teeth when told off' (Nottingham Advisory and Inspection Service, 1992:47). The report was prompted by local community groups who complained to the Commission for Racial Equality about the disproportionate numbers of Black children who were being given formal warnings, suspensions or expulsions. The ignorance of Black culture and the intolerance of some teachers were cited as possible factors in the disproportionate numbers of exclusions from Nottingham secondary schools. Fred Riddell, chairman of Nottingham Education Committee was quoted as saying that the 'problem' could be attributed to cultural misunderstanding and that:

Teachers feel threatened because Black youngsters are more exuberant than White youngsters. The way Afro-Caribbeans express their particular cultural qualities and the way they walk about school, their facial expressions, their body language, may possibly contribute more to the problem than the fact that their colour is Black (Strickland, 1991:2).

Gillborn (1990a) raises a related issue. He reports that many of the teachers in his study of an inner city school, although professing a commitment to equal opportunity and multicultural education, believed that Black pupils posed a 'threat to their authority'. This view, he argues, was rarely stated explicitly but held serious implications for relationships between White teachers and Black pupils. Teachers were often unaware of the criticism and conflict experienced by the Black child on a day-to-day basis. The result was that 'almost any display of African-Caribbean culture and identity was seen as inappropriate and therefore needing to be controlled'.

More recently, Bourne, Bridge and Searle (1994) argue that a lack of understanding of the cultural and home life of Black British pupils is leading to a disproportionate number of Black children being excluded from schools across the UK and they highlight a similar trend in denominational schools. Bourne et al urge the government to address the problem by developing a legal and moral framework for exclusion. They recommend that exclusions in the primary sector should be abolished; that all exclusions should be reviewed by independent tribunal; that an assurance be given whereby all excluded pupils receive alternative forms of tuition; and that there be an urgent review of church school exclusion policy.

Some commentators have questioned whether there is sufficient evidence to support the notion that low teacher expectations and teacher racism contribute to Black underachievement. Foster (1992a), for instance, raises the possibility that White working class and Black children may attend less 'effective' schools, which may, in turn, have an adverse effect on their attainments (see also Foster, 1990, 1991, 1992b; Hammersley and Gomm, 1993).

Irrespective of other factors in underperformance, the possibility that cultural differences in communication patterns has a negative effect on teacher perceptions of Black children cannot be dismissed. The Black child is expected to function in two languages and two cultures: one White and the other Black. However, where there is an imbalance of power, it is the person who does not hold power who is expected to adjust. When Black people do not adjust to more formal White speech or patterns of behaviour, especially in schools and courts of law, the use of the vernacular, including paralinguistic features, is often perceived as hostile and evidence of insubordination.

Differential treatment

Classroom life demands certain behaviours on the part of teacher and pupil alike. Sinclair and Coulthard (1980) for instance, identify 'initiation, feedback and response' as a linguistic structure which enables teachers to organise discourse in a ritualised form that is recognisable by pupils. The hierarchical nature of school discourse has also been observed by Fairclough (1989:38), who points to the way in which the school as a social institution not only determines discourse but can also be affected by it:

> The school has a social order and an order of discourse which involve a distinctive structuring of its 'social space' into a set of situations where discourse occurs (class, assembly, playtime, staff meeting, etc.), a set of recognised 'social roles' in which people participate in discourse (headteacher, teacher, pupil, prefect, etc.) and a set of approved purposes for discourse...The discourse types of the classroom set up subject positions for teachers and pupils, and it is only by 'occupying' these positions that one becomes a teacher or a pupil.

An understanding of the roles of teacher and pupil is crucial if effective learning is to take place. However, mismatches can occur which result in poor learning outcomes for some children. Edwards and Mercer (1987), for example, observe that:

> For many pupils, learning from teachers must appear to be a mysterious and arbitrarily difficult process, the solution to which may be to try to concentrate on trying to do and say what appears to be expected – a basically 'ritual' solution.

Studies of classroom interaction in both Britain and the USA have indicated that the experiences of Black children differ greatly from those of their White counterparts. Philips (1983), for instance, reports that African American students are disciplined in schools for speaking in loud voices. These speech patterns, she asserts, may be due to higher noise levels found in the African American community (cf Boykin, 1978).

In a similar vein, Michaels and Collins (1984:221), in an ethnographic study of classrooms, identify 'sharing time' as a key situation incorporating 'aspects of both informal home-based communication and formal discursive prose' (see also Michaels and Cazden, 1986). They assert that sharing time is a profitable area of investigation as it forms a link between the language of the home and the school. The language of the school, they argue, is closer to that of written language and, as such, can be regarded as the oral preparation for literacy. They identify two discourse styles used by Black children and White: a 'topic-associating' style which consists of a series of implicitly associated topics, frequently used by Black children, particularly Black girls; and, a 'topic-centred' style which is based on a single, clearly identifiable topic, characteristic of the White children in the study. They further report that teacher and pupil perceptions of sharing time were frequently at odds – children who adopted a 'topic-associating' style were often seen by their teachers as 'rambling'. The children, however, felt that they were being interrupted and cut short. Michaels and Collins conclude that:

> Differential treatment and negative evaluation in activities such as sharing time in part result from and also reinforce systematic differences in discourse style. In effect, some students are given instruction in how to talk in a lexically and grammatically explicit fashion, while other students are systematically excluded from that practice and instruction (p. 242).

Cazden (1988) makes similar observations in her work on American classrooms. She raises the question of whose world view needs to be challenged when assessing teacher/pupil interaction, and contends that it will take special efforts to counteract widespread and powerful patterns if all children are to benefit from effective teaching.

In Britain the work of Wright (1986, 1987) also points to patterns of differential treatment. In ethnographic studies of primary classrooms in Britain, she observes that teachers' preconceived beliefs about the educational abilities and behavioural characteristics of 'African-Caribbean' students may have an adverse effect on their eventual attainments. She identifies school processes, teacher attitudes and perceptions, and the interaction of these with pupil attitude and performance, as important considerations in the debate on Black pupils' underachievement.

Biggs and Edwards (1991) provide further support for the view that teacher interactions with Black children are different from those of their White counterparts. In their study of multi-ethnic schools they found that teachers interacted less with Black pupils and spent less time with them discussing tasks that had been set. Despite the acknowledged sensitivity of some teachers to issues of racism in the classroom, quantitative analysis indicated that some teachers 'behave in subtly different ways towards ethnic minority children' (p. 175).

In a later study, Wright (1992) observes that Black boys, in particular, are frequently singled out as the cause of disruption in the classroom, even when the same behaviours are being exhibited by other pupils. Wright further notes that peer relations between primary children are fraught with racial intolerance and teacher interactions with Black pupils highlight that:

> The Afro-Caribbean child's experience is often largely composed of expectations of bad behaviour, along with disapproval, punishment, and teacher insensitivity to the experience of racism (p. 13).

Teachers were also found to categorise students into 'types' similar to those observed by Rist (1970). Students were assigned to such groups on the basis of teacher assumptions of competence, orientation to work and behaviour. Wright concludes that teachers often held generalised images of African-Caribbeans with the result that pupils' experience of teacher interactions and expectations was frequently marked by conflict and criticism.

This position is also supported by Mac an Ghaill (1992), who, in an ethnographic study of Afro-Caribbean and Asian students in an English sixth form college, reports an awareness of the pervasive nature of racism, and the ways in which it affects schooling.

Coping and survival strategies

The process by which Black children learn to deal with the inequalities of classroom life is complex and warrants an extended treatment of its own. It is important to illustrate some of the strategies adopted by Black children in British and American classrooms and to discuss the ways in which they and Black teachers often have to compromise in order to 'succeed' in the eyes of the educational system.

It is clear from educational research that not all Black children fail to achieve high levels of academic success. Black girls, for instance, are attaining higher levels than Black boys (Mirza, 1992). Further, those of African origin are achieving better school leaving qualifications than those of Caribbean origin (Kysel, 1988; Hymas and Thomas, 1994). The question that remains, none the less, is how this success is achieved and at what cost.

Fordham and Ogbu (1986:177) in their study of a predominantly Black high school in the US, identified a 'cultural orientation' which defined academic learning in school as 'acting White' and academic success as the prerogative of White Americans. They assert that a major factor in the underachievement of Black pupils is that 'they experience inordinate ambivalence and affective dissonance with regard to academic effort and success'. In other words, to try hard is to act as though you are White and to succeed academically is to take on the dominant White values. This produces a push-pull effect, whereby many academically able Black students do not persevere or put as much effort into their schoolwork, since any display of ability is regarded as encapsulating and re-enacting the ideology of the dominant group. Consequently, many academically able students underachieve at school. They cite 'collective struggle', 'Uncle Tomming' and 'hustling' as examples of behaviours that were not congruent with success in school. Fordham and Ogbu further identified students who behaved as if they were not trying hard and acted like clowns and comedians in an effort to mask their intelligence – to be identified as a 'brainiac', the study found, was tantamount to being White. Hegarty (1989) found a similar phenomenon amongst school children in East London.

An area of related concern is reported by Fordham (1988), who observed that successful Black students adopted a 'raceless' persona in order to ensure academic success. This 'racelessness' is Fordham's term for a phenomenon whereby Black people, in an attempt to avoid the stigma of being Black, and, in order to achieve social mobility, take on attitudes, behaviours and characteristics that are not generally attributed to the Black community. It can be argued, however, that the term 'raceless' fails to explain adequately the process by which Black people reject their cultural links with the Black community and embrace the values of the dominant White ideology. I prefer to use the term 'internalised oppression', which I believe describes the experience of Black people who have not only been assimilated into a foreign culture, but have also assimilated the value and belief systems of that culture to the detriment of their individual cultural distinctiveness. This, I would argue, is common to many Black people not only in the UK and USA but more generally in the diaspora.

Fordham suggests that the quest for employment in areas that have traditionally been 'for Whites only' has meant that raceless Blacks lack identification with, or a strong relationship to the Black community. Black students, Fordham argues, are pulled by their relationship with, on the one hand, their indigenous community and, on the other, by the individualistic and competitive ideology of the American school system. 'Racelessness' and school success were inextricably linked in the students she observed, and the high achievers indicated strong beliefs in the dominant ideology of the American system. She reports that students often make choices that either put social distance between them and their peers or undermine group solidarity. A raceless persona, however, appeared to have significant value only in the school context. In short, the students had learned a form of 'internalised oppression' in order to succeed in school. Such students distanced themselves from the Black community, choosing not to identify with aspects of Black culture, language, music and dress.

A 'raceless' persona tended to be more readily adopted by girls. Female students, it appeared, were more readily predisposed to identify with the values and beliefs of the dominant society than their male counterparts. (Similar observations are made by Fuller (1980) and Mac an Ghaill (1988).) Males were less committed to the larger social system and expressed ambivalence and confusion about the value of forsaking their indigenous beliefs and values. The adoption of a raceless persona, therefore, is a pragmatic strategy. Whilst recognising that the notion of 'racelessness' cannot explain the success of all high achieving Black students, Fordham argues that this phenomenon must be further investigated if Black children's school experience is to be properly understood.

Research in the UK has, in the main, failed to recognise the strategies used by Black students in order to achieve academic success and has also failed to highlight the practice of Black teachers. An exception to this general rule, however, is described by Mac an Ghaill (1992). In a discussion of Black students' school experiences, he identifies students who 'developed a specific mode of resistance within accommodation, which involved a pro-education/anti-school perspective'. These students conformed to the demands made of them, such as working in class, completing assignments, doing homework and preparing for examinations. However, unlike anti-school students, they did not always conform to the school's social demands: the wearing of appropriate dress and hair-style, keeping silent in class, being punctual, showing respect for teachers and appearing studious and interested in lessons were not considered important. Teachers were not regarded as warranting respect or as having any great value. Rather, they were viewed as the vehicle for the acquisition of academic qualifications. The students further reported that they made friends with White teachers as a way of being sponsored through school. But this had some drawbacks. Pupils reported having to 'manage' teachers' behaviour as a way of avoiding confrontation and conflict in the classroom:

> You accept racist things to get on. You keep your head down. What choice have you? My mates knew who the racist teachers were and kept out of their way. The pupils who challenged them ended up failing. You can't win against teachers (p. 54).

Gillborn (1990b) observed similar strategies in the behaviour of Paul Dixon, a Caribbean student who had earned the label of being a 'trouble-maker' from his White teachers. By avoiding teachers with whom he was likely to be in conflict, publicly emphasising his commitment to academic achievement and accepting criticism, Paul was able to complete his latter years in secondary school and attain academic qualifications without confrontation with teachers.

What is clear from the discussion so far is that Black students have to be tactful and inventive in their interactions with White teachers, knowing how not to upset or offend, and knowing when it is acceptable to exhibit certain behaviours. Further, their experiences in the classroom indicate that they often have to suppress and deny fundamental aspects of their cultural identity in order to succeed.

Black teachers in multi-ethnic schools

The position of Black teachers in British school is best observed in relation to their dual (and often conflicting) role as members of the Black community and as agents of a system which continues to fail large numbers of Black children. Given that Black children frequently have to accommodate and make allowances for a range of implicit classroom behaviours, knowledge and skills, it could be argued that the role of the Black teacher is also influenced, and more importantly, compromised, by the same factors.

This is an area which at present remains seriously under-researched, as studies concerning Black achievement have tended to focus on the child and not the teacher. Historically, the teaching profession has represented for many people from the Caribbean the liberation from poverty and a route to increased social status. In the Caribbean, for example, education was conducted in an atmosphere of competition and a secondary education was reserved for the fortunate few who could afford it. University places and scholarships were carrots worth fighting for and were viewed as avenues for upward mobility. On arrival in the UK, however, many people from the Caribbean, including teachers, found that they could not obtain employment in the field for which they were qualified and were forced to take menial jobs as an alternative. Gilroy (1976) is one such example. In an autobiographical account of her early experiences of the British school system, she points to the overt racism and the reluctance of the education authorities to appoint her to a teaching post. Undaunted by their refusal, Gilroy persisted until she was eventually rewarded with a job at a Catholic school in North London. However, her problems did not end there. On entering her classroom for the first time, she was confronted with the following scene

> ...so when I opened the squeaking door and the class came face-to-face with me, there was a gasp of terror, then a sudden silence. A little girl broke it with a whimper. Some children visibly shook with fear, and, as I walked across the room, the whole lot − except for two boys − dived under the tables (p 47).

Such extreme examples are fortunately a thing of the past. The fact that there are documented accounts of reactions of this kind, however, underlines the fear and suspicion which has, on occasion, confronted Black people.

The plight of Black teachers has also been observed by Hubah (1984) who points to their overrepresentation in posts which offer little job security or possibilities for career advancement. She argues that the insidious nature of racism and the feeling of helplessness of many Black teachers has resulted in the dearth of Black teachers in senior positions. She also stresses the need for Black teachers to take an active role in developing educational policies.

More importantly, Hubah notes the dangers of a situation in which Black teachers fulfil 'subordinate and nondescript, mundane roles without any position of authority or status' (p 39). Firstly, this may produce a general lack of confidence on the part of the Black child and antagonistic and rebellious attitudes towards school, learning and those in positions of authority; secondly, it may lead to the same feelings of impotence on the part of Black teachers, not because of inadequate training or experience but because of the deeply engendered psychological effects of years of British colonialism. She concludes that:

> Black teachers have a formidable task ahead. We need to be dedicated and determined in our struggle to achieve equal rights and status. We need to be unified and organised if we are to succeed (p. 47).

More recently, John (1993) observes that:

> A fundamental difference between Black teachers and White teachers is that for Black teachers, the school, with all its structural arrangements, becomes a site for struggle against racism in much the same way that the community outside the school is. The experiences of racism within the society generally are replicated within the school in a wide variety of ways, in approaches to curriculum and its content, in attitudes of students, staff and parents, in the negative expectations people have of Black staff, and in the belief that it is principally the responsibility of Black staff to deal with "difficult" Black students and "awkward" Black parents.

An issue of related concern is discussed by Blair (1993), who claims that current political thinking and dominant market ideology is likely to have an adverse effect on conditions of employment for Black teachers and on educational opportunities for Black pupils. Increasing pressure on schools to create an 'image' for their consumers, she argues, means that some schools may resort to selection criteria that refer to 'ideal' consumers. Black pupils and Black teachers do not fall easily into such categories – the pupils because they are often seen as underachieving and having behavioural difficulties and the teachers because their professional competence is called into question. Many Black teachers are found in positions that have little status or security and the competitive nature of New Right market ideology do not work to their advantage. In fact, as Blair argues, it could work to their detriment by reinforcing the notion that Black teachers are 'good' at dealing with the perceived discipline problems of Black children. This de-skilling has led to an image of the Black teacher as a 'professional ethnic' (p. 15) rather than a teacher with specialised knowledge and expertise. Such stereotyping, she asserts, can also be used as the basis for assessing a Black teacher's skill. In other words, to what degree is a teacher's expertise in other areas of the curriculum 'masked by perceptions of their ethnic role?' (p. 16).

The issues for Black teachers are complex and, whilst there is no empirical evidence to indicate that the new policies will discriminate against Black teachers and pupils, events in Cleveland and Dewsbury set important precedents that could affect the selection and promotion of staff in schools. The Cleveland case involved a parent who wished to withdraw her child from a school with a 40 per cent Asian population. It was clear from the very beginning that the request to transfer was based on racial grounds. Despite the obvious racial overtones of the case, Cleveland local education authority agreed with the parents' wishes to transfer the child to a school with a predominantly White population. A judicial review held four years later upheld the LEA's decision, arguing that provision for parental choice under the 1988 Education Reform Act (ERA) took precedence over the 1976 Race Relation Act under which a decision of this kind had previously been illegal. Shortly afterwards, another parent in Dewsbury was allowed to withdraw her child from a multi-ethnic school, thus setting the pattern for future decisions of this kind. More important for the purposes of the present discussion, the ERA also enables schools and governors to exercise 'choice' over the recruitment, selection, promotion and retention of teachers. Given the evidence outlined above, there are real concerns that Black teachers may suffer unduly under the new legislation.

The role of Black teachers in the 1990s and in the years to come will be a crucial one. The presence of Black British teachers, as well as Caribbean-born teachers recruited through access courses, licensed teachers schemes and the like, will undoubtedly have an effect on the eventual outcomes of the Black child. We have only just begun to scratch the surface of a critical issue in the debate on Black achievement. The cumulative effects of recent changes to educational thinking, decreasing numbers of ethnic minority teachers and the imposition of a eurocentric curriculum will add to the many difficulties that already exist for many Black children and teachers in British schools (Guy and Menter, 1992; Blair and Maylor, 1993).

Conclusion

This chapter has looked at the role of culture in the schooling of African origin pupils in both the USA and UK. It has also highlighted the position of Black teachers and children in the British educational system.

Particular attention has been given to the ways in which aspects of cultural style, and, in particular, non-verbal behaviour, can operate in direct opposition to the authority structure of schools. This often results in negative teacher perceptions of Black pupils and in disproportionate numbers of suspensions, exclusions and referrals to off-site units for Black pupils, especially boys.

There is no shortage of evidence that Black children behave in culturally different ways and that these differences are often perceived negatively by White teachers. In recent years, however, a growing body of research, particularly in the USA, has clarified how these negative views are translated into teacher behaviours which help to perpetuate educational underachievement by Black pupils. Equally pertinent is the research on the coping strategies developed by Black children in order to manage the behaviours of teachers and which guarantee their academic success.

Chapter 5

Black communications:
African retained language patterns in multi-ethnic classrooms

In the previous chapter we saw some of the ways in which Black cultural style is misinterpreted by White teachers. Here we look in greater detail at what precisely constitutes this cultural style, focusing particularly on African retentions in the diaspora. Drawing on discussion of these retentions in the literature and on actual examples observed during fieldwork in two primary schools, attention is paid to call-response, 'signifying', repetition, moral teachings and various forms of non-verbal communication which, collectively, have been labelled by writers such as Hoover (1985) and Dandy (1991) as 'Black Communications'.

Patterns of communication

Many writers have commented on the presence of African derived practices in new world communities. Hilliard (1985:155), for instance, argues that:

> Africans in the African diaspora, including the Americans and the Caribbeans retained and still retain varying degrees of African culture. The culture is reflected in family patterns, language, religious belief systems, artistic creativities, etc.

Writing on a similar theme, Taylor (1990), observes similarities that exist in the rhythms, gestures, and movements created by Africans. Mythaphonics – the combination of speech, music, dance and non-verbal communication – he argues, are found in African communities throughout the new world. Black Communications comprise a complex system of verbal and non verbal interactions (outlined in Figure 1).

I analysed some sixty hours of video-recorded classroom interactions were to establish whether 'Black Communications' were a feature of Black teachers' style. Three distinctively Black patterns of communication were observed: call-response, signification and repetition.

Call-response

Call-response is major characteristic of oral cultures and is prevalent in many African and Caribbean communities. Its use has also been widely documented throughout the diaspora. Writers such as Sutcliffe and Tomlin (1986), Callender and Cameron (1990) and Tomlin (1994), for instance, have commented on its use in Britain, whilst Smitherman (1977), Rosenburg (1988) and Mitchell (1970; 1990) have written extensively on the subject in America. Call-response is the principle organising characteristic of African communication. Smitherman (1977:104), describes it as

> ... spontaneous verbal and non-verbal interaction between speaker and listener in which all of the speaker's statements ('calls') are punctuated by expressions ('responses') from the listener.

Responses can occur during or after the call and can be both verbal and non-verbal. This 'contrapuntal' effect can sometimes lead those who are unfamiliar with Black discourse to describe the language as anarchic and disorganised (Reisman, 1974).

Although call-response can be observed in many different kinds of Black discourse, it is particularly conspicuous in the rhetoric of the Black church. Preachers, for example, are regularly observed calling upon the congregation to reply to the words of the sermon. It is also found in Black musical forms such as Reggae, Soca, Calypso, Ragga, Blues, Soul and Jazz. Writing about the presence of call-response in Black music Holloway (1991:193), observes that:

> The call-response structure is the key mechanism that allows for the manipulation of time, text and pitch. The response or repetitive chorus provides a stable foundation for the improvised lines of the soloist. The use of call-response structures to generate musical change has been described many times in Black music literature.

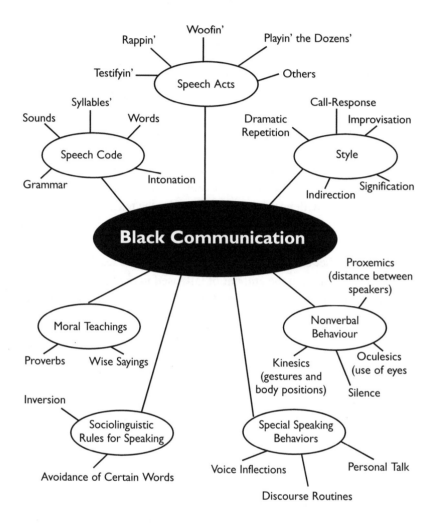

**Figure 1: Black Communications is not just a speech code.
It is a system of communication** (from EAB Dandy 1991)

Call-response in an educational setting

American research has pointed to differences in Black children's language in the home and school. Lein (1975:3), for example, observed the ways in which Black children use many characteristically Black language patterns at home, whilst at school they are less inclined to display such patterns. In a study of the speech behaviour and linguistic styles of Black American migrant children, she found that in the home 'children talk with adults, play verbal games with them, and argue with them, although usually in joking terms', whereas at school their discourse 'often involves long monologues with limited participation by others'. She observed the children in four settings: at home with their parents; at home with no adults; supervised by the teacher at school and unsupervised at school. Her findings suggest that the migrant children spoke less in the supervised classroom and scored even lower when compared to other students described as 'able' by the teacher. Lein also points to differences in the amount of talk used in the home and school. For example, Black children were found to talk more with peers and less with adults.

Along similar lines, Young (1970) points to a 'contest' type of speech between Black mothers and their children. Speech, she asserts, is volleyed rhythmically and children are encouraged to be assertive and develop a style of their own. Teachers who use rhythm in speech and engage in verbal rapport with Black children, she claims, may connect culturally with those who interact rhythmically with their mothers at home.

Where aspects of Black Communications have been adopted in the classroom, writers have noted that reading attainment and pupil participation are increased. Piestrup (1974) (cited in Hale-Benson), for example, identified techniques utilised in reading by children who spoke Black dialect. Particularly noteworthy is her discussion of the 'Black Artful' style displayed by pupils with high reading proficiency. These children had been taught by a Black teacher 'who used dialect with them, spoke rhythmically, used varied intonation and engaged in verbal interplay'. The use of repetition, call-response and alliteration were observed – features which occur naturally in the oral traditions of African communities. A high degree of rapport was also evident in the teachers' lesson as well as a high level of involvement by the students.

Foster (1989) also comments on Black language patterns in her ethnographic study of an American teacher. She notes that the teacher uses a range of strategies in the classroom – particularly marked are the times when discussion becomes lively and there is a high degree of student participation. Such instances are labelled *performances* because they closely resembled Black preaching style and expressive talk. Foster observes that the teacher 'specifically calls for active, vocal audience response' (p. 14). The stylised and interactive nature of the speech event is noticeable for the use of prosodic features such as vowel elongation, changes in meter and tempo and single speaker repetition. Foster concludes that:

> In spite of the fact that the talk resembles play, the focus of these performances is instructional... and it is through performances that explanations and learning take place (p. 20).

Similar patterns are also observed in the teaching style of Marva Collins, a Black American educator noted for her success in raising the attainments of Black pupils in Chicago (Hollins, 1982; Collins and Tamarkin, 1982).

Call-response in British classrooms

Call-response patterns vary according to their intent. Smitherman (1977: 107), for instance, identifies five types of call-response: *cosigning* – which refers to behaviours which affirm or agree with the speaker; *encouraging* – in which the speaker is urged to continue in the direction they are going; *repetition* – where the words of the speaker are repeated; *completer responses* – which complete the speakers statements either in direct response to a request from the speaker or in spontaneous talk with the speaker; and, finally *'On T'* responses – which are powerful co-signing responses which acknowledge that something has been said right on time, that is 'psychological time'.

In the present study call-response was evident amongst three of the teachers. The most frequently occurring patterns were: co-signing, completer and On T responses.

Co-signing responses

Co-signing responses are those which confirm or endorse a speaker's words or actions. The following extract taken from Martin Luther

King's *I Have a Dream* speech shows how the audience affirm King's calls as he leads the participants to a dramatic climax:

King:	I have a dream that one day even the state of Mississippi, a desert sweltering with the heat of injustice and oppression
Audience:	Yeah, yeah
King:	will be transformed into an oasis of freedom and justice
Audience:	Amen, amen [the audience start to applaud]
King:	I have a dream that my four little children
Audience:	Amen, amen, yeah, yeah
King:	Will one day live in a nation where they will not be judged by the colour of their skin but by the content of their character
Audience:	[the amens increase in intensity and the applause grows]

The audience who respond spontaneously affirm King's sentiments in very clear terms.

In the present study co-signing responses were observed in Mrs Adesanya's classroom. Take, for instance, the following. Mahogany, a Black girl in Year five, is reading. She finds reading difficult and is very reluctant. She nonetheless perseveres to the end of the book. Mrs Adesanya is obviously pleased and announces to the class:

Mahogany has successfully read a level two book. She is now ready for level three. Let us congratulate Mahogany, we should all clap for her [the class applaud Mahogany].

In this example the class respond to Mrs Adesanya's direct call by applauding Mahogany, therefore affirming Mrs Adesanya's statement: 'She is now ready for level three'.

On another occasion Bryan, a Black boy in the class, has volunteered to read a passage to the class. He reads well and uses a range of intonation to inform and engage the listener. Mrs Adesanya has made explicit to the children the standards they need to attain for each reading level in the National Curriculum. For instance, she is often heard telling the children, 'A level three child knows how to listen and can explain what has been read' and 'A level four child uses paragraphs and punctuation'. When Bryan has finished she remarks:

Mrs Adesanya:	Very good, well read.
	[To class] What level can we give Bryan's reading?
Pupils:	Level one
	Level four
Mrs Adesanya:	How do you know it's four, Genesis?
Genesis:	Fluent miss
Mrs Adesanya:	Pardon. He read fluently. What other reason? What other word can we add about his reading? He read with what? Expression
Pupils:	Yes

In this case the pupils concur with Mrs Adesanya's assessment of Bryan's achievement. The marked use of call-response as part of Mrs Adesanya's repertoire clearly reflect her origins in West Africa, where such patterns exist as a part of everyday communication.

Completer responses

Completer responses complete a speaker's statement, occur in response to a request or, occasionally, occur as a spontaneous act in talk with another speaker. For example, at a Pentecostal church in South London, a testifier talks about his life prior to joining the church:

Testifier:	Repentance is when you turn from what you are doing. Before I got saved I was, I was
Pastor:	No good
Testifier:	No good, yes. Thank you pastor.

In the present study completer responses were again most often found in Mrs Adesanya's class. Take, for instance, the following extract where the children have been painting famous characters from Victorian England. She is walking around the classroom observing the children's work when she suddenly declares to no one in particular:

Mrs Adesanya (call): Be very careful OK. We want it to be the best. Nothing but the

Pupils (response):   best

Mrs Adesanya: best

The pupils respond spontaneously to Mrs Adesanya's call. The call-response pattern which she uses serves to merge teacher and pupils into an educative whole and indicates the shared knowledge of this strategy which exists in her classroom. There is no distinction between speaker and responder: communication is effective because everyone takes part.

Completer responses also occurred in response to a direct call from the teacher to the whole class. The following took place when Mrs Adesanya's class were being video-recorded. Peter, a White child in year five, is 'acting' for the camera and encouraging others to join him. The class are decorating the covers of their project folders entitled 'Plants and Animals'. Peter is seen by Mrs Adesanya, who asks:

Mrs Adesanya: Peter Elliot can you sit down for a while? Ask yourself what am I doing. Can you ask yourself what am I doing? Am I just doing it like a two year old and scribbling it just like this? What are all these?

Peter: Background

Mrs Adesanya: What are all these?

Peter: Background

Mrs Adesanya: Background of what?

[By this time the rest of the class have noticed and are looking towards Peter's desk. Mrs Adesanya picks the work up and holds it up for the class]

Mrs Adesanya: Children can you listen, can you listen. What did I ask you to do on this cover? [The children

	now see Peter's folder and respond with cries of uuggh!]
Tesfa:	You asked us to draw plants and animals
Mrs Adesanya (call):	Plants and what?
All (response):	Animals
Mrs Adesanya:	Animals

The class, who are familiar with the use of completers, punctuate Mrs Adesanya's' calls with appropriate responses – what begins as an individual inquiry becomes a group activity where all members affirm the purpose of the task. However, not all cases of completer responses involved the whole class. Here, Mrs Adesanya calls for Andre, a Black boy, to respond. He does so spontaneously:

Mrs Adesanya (call):	When you are doing something like this, you use your brain. Use your what?
Andre (response):	Brain
Mrs Adesanya:	Brain

Rapport exists between Mrs Adesanya and the children. The use of call-response emphasises shared knowledge and group norms. The overriding impression of her classroom is one of harmony, spontaneity and mutual understanding.

'On T' responses

'On T' are powerful co-signing responses which serve to affirm speaker behaviour as well as acknowledge the fact that what has been said occurs at precisely the right moment. Smitherman (1977:107) suggests that such responses can include phrases such as, 'shonuff, yassuh and gon wit yo bad self', and non-verbal actions where 'the hands are waved in the air; giving five; jumping up; hollering and clapping hands'. These responses signify the timeliness of a statement or action, so giving the speaker immediate feedback on the merit of their contribution.

In the following, Mr Thompson is observed using an 'On T' response. Julian is at the board working on a maths problem. Much to the amusement of his peers, it is wrong and he has made several attempts to correct it. He finally gets it right and looks to his teacher for a sign of acknowledgement. Mr Thompson remains straight-faced. He looks towards the class and asks:

Mr Thompson: Is that correct?

Pupils: Yes

Mr Thompson: Yes, Julian [he starts to clap and the class follow]

This illustrates not only the way the pupils respond to Mr Thompson's call but also the teacher's enthusiastic response to Julian's achievement.

'On T' responses were also observed in the classroom of another teacher. Kasru, an Asian pupil, is asked to name a noun in the sentence, 'The sheep were in the field'. Kasru is finding it difficult so Mr Wiltshire invites him to name an object that he can find at home.

Kasru: Table

Mr Wiltshire: Look at the board and give me a noun in the sentence

Kasru: Sheep [the class spontaneously applaud Kasru]

The class respond without prompting from the teacher and Kasru is given immediate confirmation that his response is not only correct but also timely. In sum, call-response which occurs in many spheres of Black culture, encourages group participation and the establishment of shared norms. In the educational setting it can also be utilised to positively reinforce pupil knowledge.

Signifying

Signifying is a way of humourously putting down another person in a conversation which usually involves an element of indirection (Mitchell-Kernan, 1972; Smitherman, 1977). Take the following example of signifying in a group of African-American adolescents reported by Smitherman (1977:118):

Sherry: I sho hongy. Dog!

Reginald: That's all you think bout, eating all the time.

John [Sherry's brother]:   Man, that's why she so big.

Sherry:	Aw, y'all shut up!
John:	Come on, Sherry, we got to go. We'll catch you later, man.
Reginald [to John]:	Goodnight. Sleep tight
	Don't let Sherry,
	Eat you up tonight.

Reginald has substituted the words of the rhyme 'Goodnight, sleep tight, don't let the bed bugs bite' with signification on Sherry. Although he does not refer to Sherry directly he still manages to comment on her large appetite. Smitherman concludes that signifying is 'characterised by exploitation of the unexpected and quick verbal surprises' (p. 119).

My study noted signifying in the classrooms of two teachers. Mr Wiltshire, who has dismissed his class for break, is waiting for a group of girls to leave the classroom. He is perched on his desk with a metre stick in his hand – which he often used in a playful way as a warning to the children. Nakeisha, who is Black, is taking her time to leave the classroom. When she eventually gets to the door Mr Wiltshire calls her and says

> ... Nakeisha take care. You know you must respect what I have in my hand

Nakeisha is being told in a roundabout way that if she does not leave the room quickly her teacher may have reason to use the metre stick. As expected, she makes her departure swiftly.

On another occasion, Seanne, who is in Mr Thompson's class, asks for permission to leave the room.

Seanne:	Can I go to the toilet sir?
Mr Thompson:	There's a bucket in the corner

Mr Thompson could quite easily have said 'no'. Instead he suggests an alternative which is so bizarre that Seanne is left with no doubt that the answer is a negative one. Seanne's peers also play a part in the process of signifying on him. On hearing Mr Thompson's response some of them exclaim, 'You've been told'.

Repetition

Repetition in Black discourse is highly valued and is apparent in all levels of communication. Edwards and Sienkewicz (1990:143), for instance, argue that repetition serves three functions. It can be used, firstly as a device which stimulates involvement; secondly, as a reminder of the talk that has gone before; and lastly, as an opportunity for speakers to gather their thoughts before going on. Writing on the use of repetition in the Black idiom, Smitherman (1977:142) observes that:

> Key words and sounds are repeated in succession, both for emphasis and effect. Believing that meaningful sounds can move people, the Black speaker capitalises on effective uses of repetition.

The words of Malcolm X illustrate the way in which the alliteration, or the repetition of initial sounds can be used to bring home an important message. For example, during the 1960s he warned Americans in the South that there could either be 'voting or violence' and that desegregation could be achieved through 'the ballot or the bullet'. Keywords and phrases represent another effective use of repetition in speech. The following extract from the 1984 American Presidential campaign shows how Jesse Jackson repeats the sentence, 'I am somebody', on three occasions. Each time a segment of the sentence is repeated, audience participation heightens, until gradually, the intensity of the message leads the audience to a moving crescendo.

Jackson:	I am	(loud)
Audience:	I am	(loud)
Jackson:	Somebody	(loud)
Audience:	Somebody	(loud)
Jackson:	I am	(loud)
Audience:	I am	(loud)
Jackson:	Somebody	(louder)
Audience:	Somebody	(louder)
Jackson:	I am	(louder)
Audience:	I am	(louder)
Jackson:	Somebody	(very loud)
Audience:	Somebody	(very loud)
Jackson:	Somebody	(very loud)
Audience:	Somebody	(very loud)

Piestrup (1974) and Foster (1989) also observe the use of repetition in the classrooms of Black teachers, and argue that it represents culturally familiar speech which is recognised by members of a speech community who share similar norms. In the present study, the use of repetition was a particular feature of Mrs Adesanya's teaching style. In the following extract, she asks Bryan, a Black boy, to work at another table as he is off-task. She notices that, despite his removal from his usual place of work, he is still not concentrating and inquires as to his achievements for the day. Note the emphasis placed on the word *move*.

> How far are you working? Can I see what you have achieved? [Bryan turns the page of his book] Get up again and move to that table. Pack your trouble. Move to that table please. Move to that table and if I move you again you move outside.

The rhythmic manner in which the message is delivered is similar to that of chanting in a song.

Mrs Campbell also used dramatic repetition as part of her repertoire. In the following example she notices that Charles is engaged in task avoidance behaviour. She announces:

Mrs Campbell:	Please get up from that seat. Leave that seat please and go away. Go and use your brain. Find another seat. Please just go.
Charles:	Where to Miss?
Mrs Campbell:	Just find another seat

Charles is left in no doubt that his teacher wants him to sit in another part of the room. The repeated use of phrases: find another seat, leave that seat, etc fully reinforce his teacher's message. Repetition was also used to remind pupils of their teachers' expectations whilst at school. In my observations of Mrs Adesanya's class she frequently asked the children, 'What have you achieved today?' In the following example, Jaydeen is talking to Anita. Mrs Adesanya says to Jaydeen

> ...what do you want there? Go away, she wants... I want her to *achieve*. Please just excuse me, move away from there. She will *achieve*. Just go away, I want her to *achieve*.

Emphasis is placed on 'achieve' and Jaydeen is implicitly told that she is impeding Anita's prospects. Students were also encouraged to question their actions and those of others through the use of repetition. Take, for instance, the following example, where Mrs Adesanya notices that Joseph is not totally immersed in his task of painting. He is looking around at a group of pupils nearby. She sees him and says

> Can you tell them to be quiet because they are talking. If you are a real artist you need to look at them as fools. Do you need to listen to them? Do you need to? Do you need to?

Repetition of the question 'Do you need to?' reinforces the point that Joseph must concentrate if he is to achieve his best. One effect of this type of questioning is that Joseph is forced to focus on the need to pay attention. Note, too, the similarity to Proverbs, chapter three, verse thirty-five: 'The wise shall inherit glory; but shame will be the promotion of fools'. The use of proverbial expression is another feature of Black Communications and it is to a discussion of this that I now turn.

Moral teachings

Another important feature of Black discourse is the use of proverbs and wise sayings. Smitherman (1977:95) describes proverbs as 'short succinct statements which have the sound of wisdom and power'. Proverbs are widely used in African and Caribbean communities and in other parts of the diaspora. Achebe (1980:7), for instance, claims that

> ...among the Ibo the art of conversation is regarded very highly, and proverbs are the palm-oil with which the words are eaten.

Roberts (1988: 157) makes similar observations about proverbs in the Caribbean. Their use, he suggests, 'is a direct legacy of their great importance in African societies'. Mbiti (1990) also points to the use of African proverbs. He argues that they are a traditional way of expressing religious ideas and philosophical wisdom.

The short statements are easily remembered and can be passed on to others. Smitherman, too, points to the use of proverbs in child rearing and argues that they function as a teaching device where the mother's intention is to impress upon the child a specific point (cf Boateng, 1980). 'If you can't hear you must feel' is a common proverb used by older Black people to children who do not listen or heed warnings, the implication being that failure to listen results in difficulty. Jackson (1986:32) argues that proverbs are 'designed to teach in all walks of life, especially to children'. He cites several Jamaican derived proverbs that are found in the British context, for example:

> See and blind, hear and deaf – which is a way of advocating discretion: whatever you see or hear, it is best to mind your own business.

Their use is largely unidirectional – young people do not generally use proverbs to their elders. This view is supported by Edwards and Sienkewicz (1990) who note that, in Yoruba society, linguistic etiquette requires a younger person to preface a proverb to an elder with an apology. This, they claim, 'acknowledges the central role which proverbs play in children's education'(p. 170).

Edwards and Sienkewicz also assert that proverbial expression displays community values at the same time as allowing the speaker to make indirect statements. It is possible, therefore, for a speaker to be critical and to make a point politely without passing direct comment. This feature enables the speaker to depersonalise a statement. These writers point, too, to the need to study proverbial strategies in their contexts. For, where proverbs occur as decontextualised texts, they effectively

> ...leave unclear the proverbs' meanings' within the culture and tempt readers to impose from their own culture interpretations which may or may not be appropriate (p. 169).

In an autobiographical description, Marva Collins recounts how she uses proverbs in her classroom practice as a way of instilling in children the value of education. The following excerpt gives a flavour of Collins' highly individual teaching style and how proverbs are used in her classroom. Opening the text to the underlined passages, Marva quoted:

> Proverbs, Chapter 3, verse 35 says 'Honor is the portion of wise men, but fools inherit shame.' Chapter 6, verse 6: 'Go to the ant, O sluggard, study her ways and learn wisdom.' Chapter 10, verse 4: 'The slack hand impoverishes, but the hand of the diligent enriches'.' Marva paused and looked out at the children.
>
> 'What do you think those proverbs mean?'...
>
> 'Cindy, would you please tell us what they mean?'

'A lazy person will be poor and won't have anything,' Cindy blurted out quickly, repeating one of her mother's pet phrases

(Collins and Tamarkin, 1982: 85-86).

Heath (1983) also points to children's interpretation of proverbs in her study of Trackton and Roadville. She notes that the pre-school children of Roadville were able to interpret proverbs without necessarily understanding their literal meanings and were able to alter their behaviours accordingly. Further, she asserts that proverbs only make sense where cultural experience is shared.

Ladson-Billings and Henry (1990:80), in a study of successful teachers of Black children in America and Canada, also report the use of proverbs as a part of regular classroom practice. Ese, one of the teachers involved in the study, used proverbs as a way of 'making connections with a collective cultural memory'.

As we have seen, proverbial expressions can act as an educative tool whereby teachers can transmit shared values to the group. In the present study, three of the six Black teachers were observed using proverbial expressions or wise sayings in the classroom. One that was often heard when children were inattentive was 'If you can't listen, you won't learn'.

Its intention is explicit. Similarly, when Ken is distracting another pupil at his table, teacher Pearlette Campbell, looks at him and says: 'Disruption and education do not mix together'. Ken, who obviously understands the intention of Pearlette's message, stops what he is doing and gets on with reading his book. This proverb is equally applicable to other class members and acts as a caution: if they wish to achieve educationally they should not be disruptive.

Teachers also invoked wise sayings to encourage children not to mimic the actions of others. Take Wesley, a White pupil in year six taught by Leroy Wiltshire at Haling Park school. The class have recently visited the Science Museum and are writing up a report on their visit. Wesley has allowed himself to be distracted by Tesfa and is talking to him. Unbeknown to them, Mr Wiltshire has been watching them. After a few minutes, he declares:

Mr Wiltshire: Wesley I used to think you were a serious boy

Wesley:	What sir?
Mr Wiltshire:	Monkey see, monkey do

The essence of this proverb is that if someone behaves or acts in a certain way it does not necessarily mean that you should follow. In short, you should know your own mind. Wesley appears to understand the intention of Mr Wiltshire's remark, as he does not ask for clarification, nor does he continue his conversation with Tesfa.

Mrs Sargeant also used proverbs to the children in her class. Barry has been asked to move to another table. He objects and persists in asking his teacher 'Why?' Mrs Sargeant replies: 'Eyebrow is longer than beard'. This proverb has its origins in the Caribbean. It is designed to curb questions from children, reminding them that they should not challenge the wisdom of adults. It can be used in two closely related ways: firstly, with young children who are considered impertinent, its essence being that they should not question adults who know best; secondly, with older children, who are reminded that, although they may have grown up, they still have a lot to learn. In short, eyebrows grow before beards.

Another feature of Black discourse style is the use of riddles. Riddles, like proverbs, are an important part of African oral tradition. There are, however, differences between the two events. Edwards and Sienkewicz (1990) note that the point of a proverb can be deduced from the context in which it occurs, whereas a riddle has to provide its own referent. The purpose of riddles, they assert, is 'to entertain by creating a confusion which is eventually resolved by supplying an answer to the question' (p. 172). Roberts (1988:155), writing about riddles in the Caribbean, states that riddles resemble 'a linguistic puzzle with an unusual solution'. He also points to specific formulae which are found at the beginning and ending of riddles, for instance, that Jamaican riddles often start with the following formula: 'Riddle me this, riddle me that, Guess me this riddle and perhaps not', followed by the question, 'What is that?'

Riddles did not occur as part of the normal events in the classrooms studied. But we can see how Mr Thompson used Jamaican riddling formula to demonstrate a complex phenomenon – the function of the retina. The class had been studying parts of the eye and the way they work. The children made model retinas using hollow tubes, tissue paper and foil. When they looked through the tubes, the images appeared upside-down. Mr Thompson explains that it was the brain which corrected the images so that objects appear the right way up. It is an unusual concept and some of the class are finding it difficult to grasp. He finally declares:

Mr Thompson:	When you look in the mirror what do you see? Is the left on the left or on the right?
Pupils:	The right
Mr Thompson: the	Good. So, if you are standing up, the foot is in head and the head is in the foot. [The children laugh] When you go home tonight ask your mother this. Riddle me this, riddle me that. Guess me this riddle and perhaps not. What is when the head is in the foot and the foot is in the head? Now does everybody understand?

Mr Thompson uses the riddling formula to explain a complex occurrence to the children. Initially this causes confusion. However, when they eventually understand the explanation, they respond by laughing.

Creole usage

In their study of successful teachers of Black students, Ladson-Billings and Henry (1990:82) highlight the use of pupil's home language as a medium for and the content of instruction:

> When the teachers use the home language of Black students to teach, they are employing a strategy of culturally relevant teaching which exemplifies a reversal of the accepted canon of appropriate English to be used in the class. Caribbean and/or Black English can be both the medium and the content of instruction.

Teachers in the present study used Creole in two ways – either as part of humourous interchange with students or as part of their reprimanding behaviour. Take this scenario in Mr Wiltshire's class. The class have been working on nouns. Tevin, a Black boy, has put his hand up several times and finally Mr Wiltshire urges him to allow someone else to answer. He asks the class:

Mr Wiltshire:	Are there any other nouns in that sentence? [Tevin's hand shoots up into the air and he has a grin on his face. Mr Wiltshire ignores him. Tevin calls out]
Tevin:	Sir, Sir
Mr Wiltshire:	Yuh can' hear. I tell yuh, don' call me [The class including Tevin and Mr Wiltshire laugh]

Deborah Lashley, talking about her use of Creole with pupils observed:

> I cuss them in Patois more. If they've got any sense, they don't want to take the shame.

Pupils were conscious of their teachers' use of Creole. Although none of the pupils commented directly, many used Creole in reporting what their teachers had said. For example, Mr Wiltshire, often tells children to kneel on the floor with their hands on their heads or to stand on their chairs when reprimanding them. When asked how Mr Wiltshire tells him off, Andrew, a Black boy, replied:

> ... Look ere. Stop de talkin. Kneel down, put yuh han pon yuh head. Up pon de chair.

And Cherylle, a pupil in Pearlette Campbell's class, reports that her teacher says: 'Sit down bwoy. Sit down gyal'.

Or take the case of Mr Thompson when revising ratios. He is waiting for the class to respond to his question. The children have not grasped the concept. Mr Thompson is walking about the room checking on individual students. Dave, a Black pupil, calls to Mr Thompson who ignores him and instead leans on a cupboard on the far side of the classroom. He is watching the students intently. Suddenly he speaks, pointing towards Felicia:

> ...when I come to yuh, yuh see yuh better have everyting right.

Mrs Campbell also used Creole as part of her reprimanding behaviour. When Ken is off task. Mrs Campbell looks at him and says:

> ... sid down bwoy. Ken read my lips. If yuh don go an sid down I'm going to give you back de money for de trip tomorrow.

Mr Wiltshire was similarly observed using mesolectal varieties with children. He uses standard Trinidadian creole habitually but on occasions switches to a broader variety. Here we see him teaching the children about Dr Harold Moody as part of Black history month. A girl from another class comes to the door and while he is attending to her query, the children become unsettled and start to talk. The noise level gradually increases. When he is finished he turns back to the class and says:

> ... all yuh is talkin when yuh ain suppose to be talkin. Yuh is talkin when yuh ain suppose to be talkin. All yuh can stan up. Stan up.

A range of characteristically Black verbal strategies, then, is observed among teachers in the study. Also noted are a number of non-verbal and paralinguistic cues, and it is to a discussion of these that we now turn.

Non-verbal communication

Non-verbal cues are an essential part of effective interaction, and the way in which the body is used to deliver messages often shows how people feel. Miller (1990, cited in Dandy, 1991) for instance, suggests that as much as 93 per cent of the communication which takes place amongst American teachers and pupils is non-verbal. She further asserts that African Americans rely heavily on non-verbal cues 'which accompany and confirm verbal communications'. Miller concludes that teachers should not only be aware of the messages they send to students but also of the messages students are sending to them. Incorrect interpretation of such messages can lead to mistrust.

Both teachers and pupils are involved in the communication process. Discord arises when there are gaps in the knowledge that each party has of the other's repertoire. Taylor (1990:1) provides a useful explanation of the interrelationship between culture and communication in the school:

> Everything that occurs within a school, and especially in the classroom, involves communication, the act of sharing information. Sometimes communication involves the use of oral or written **verbal** symbols. On other occasions, communication involves various types of **nonverbal** symbols, including body language... Most behaviour problems in schools, and their resolutions, involve some type of communication. In sum, communication

permeates education. Communication is culture bound. The way an individual communicates emanates from his or her culture... one basic truth prevails: communication is a product of culture.

Three areas of non-verbal communication are particularly noteworthy here; body language, the use of eyes and paralinguistic features.

Body language

We saw in chapter four that research on differential treatment of non-White children in British schools has shown that Black pupils' body language has been misinterpreted and often leads to suspension and expulsion (CRE, 1985; Nottingham Advisory and Inspection Service, 1992; Gillborn, 1988, 1990b; Bourne, Bridge and Searle, 1994).

Although these studies highlight an important feature of the day-to-day experiences of Black children in school, they have tended to concentrate on their perceived negative behaviours and the way in which these affect their relationships with teachers and the school. Very little research in Britain has attempted to interpret these behaviours or to analyse them from a Black perspective. Nor has the extent to which Black teachers use aspects of Black communications in the classroom been investigated in a British context.

Particular aspects of non-verbal behaviour are characteristic of the Black community. Cooke (1980), for instance, suggests that stances carry significant meaning in Black Communications. Such stances often accompany verbal strategies such as rapping or woofing. Rapping relies on the skill of the speaker to engage and entertain the listener. A rap is successful if it absorbs the listener. Rappers perform using a range of non-verbal cues and a range of intonation in the delivery of their performance. Woofing refers to a form of bragging or boasting which is often misinterpreted by members of other cultures. It aims to sustain anger at the verbal level and relieve tension in lieu of a fight. Hale-Benson (1982: 171) observes that:

> Through woofing, a player can maintain an image of being fearless and tough with the hope that once that image is achieved, he won't have to prove it.

Writing about this verbal routine, Kochman (1981) notes that Whites often regard hostile words and violent actions as one and the same, whereas Blacks conceive them to be different things. The dramatic dimension of woofing, he argues, renders it as acting, therefore its function is reduced to play.

According to the woofing routine, when the challenge is accepted the speaker has sold a 'woof ticket'. A major characteristic of woofing is that speakers do not woof on someone whom they cannot beat, frighten or intimidate. So for woofing to be successful, the recipient is on the defensive and the speaker on the offensive.

These stances may also include a hard look or what has been labelled 'the showdown'. Writers such as Kunjufu (1986a, 1986b), Dandy (1991) and Dent (1989) have argued that when a Black student stands with arms folded and stares at a White teacher, the student has the psychological advantage. The setting, the strategy and the conclusion have already been defined by the student. In short, the teacher is considered 'powerless' in the interaction. The student seems to be saying 'I'm bad and I know I'm bad'. However, when an adult in the Black community adopts a similar stance – perhaps standing with hands akimbo, or, with both hands on the hips – they are saying 'I mean business' 'stop what you are doing' or 'you're in big trouble' (Dandy, 1991:37).

Writing on White teacher relationships with Black boys in America, Kunjufu (1986; 1987; 1989) asserts that the body language of Black boys is often misinterpreted by White teachers. He argues that when a Black boy stares defiantly at his teachers he is not necessarily challenging their authority. The 'showdown', a form of woofing, is inextricably linked with Black boys' rites of passage to manhood. The showdown is not always a match of strength against strength. For Black boys there may also be issues relating to peer approval, attitudes to discipline, desire for knowledge and expectations of adults which lead them to 'test' the genuineness of their teachers. Of particular interest are Kunjufu's photographs, one of which shows Black boys with their arms folded across their chests and a steady gaze, and the other using animated body positions in a school hallway. These same behaviours are a cause of chagrin for many teachers. Kunjufu suggests that it is more profitable to devise strategies to deal with them and to explain their historical significance than trying to contain them.

I observed Black teachers using similar stances to those described by Kunjufu as a means of controlling misbehaviour. Take Pearlette Campbell, who has been watching Ken, a Black boy. The class are doing silent reading and Ken appears to be taking his time in the selection of a book.

> [Pearlette stands and watches with her arms akimbo] Ken are you getting a book or what?
>
> [She folds both hands across her chest]
>
> Just get your book and read it
>
> [She stands, arms folded, with her eyes fixed on Ken].

It is helpful to look at this example in more detail. The initial stance adopted by Mrs Campbell communicates her frustration to Ken. In short, she is saying, 'I'm getting angry with you.' She then asks him what his intentions are whilst simultaneously saying, 'I mean business.' Finally, she combines her stance with a hard look. By this time, Ken is fully aware of Mrs Campbell's displeasure. He responds by quickly selecting a book. The combination of stance and the use of a fixed stare was an effective form of communication in this case.

Body language was also used to communicate agreement. I was observing Mr Wiltshire's class when the pupils were working on plurals. Edward has pluralised the sentence, 'The ladies preferred roses.' Mr Wiltshire remarks

Mr Wiltshire:	Good. Edward knows what to do. Tevin, what do you have to do?
Tevin:	I'll buy them for my girls [the class laugh]
Mr Wiltshire:	Yes, very well

He then moves over to Tevin and signals that they should 'touch'. This occurs where two or more parties roll their fists and the knuckles are touched with those of the other participants. In the British context, touching is used in a similar way to 'giving skin' in America, and is a way of communicating unity and oneness. Cooke (1980), writing in America, explains that giving skin is a practice usually observed in male domains and can act as a symbolic greeting instead of a handshake; as a way of saying hello or goodbye; to show approval or agreement; proposal or suggestion; or as a form of congratulation on an impressive statement. Its major significance lies in the way it strengthens and reaffirms group solidarity.

Use of eyes

Rickford and Rickford (1976) observe that in African and Caribbean communities, the eyes can be used to communicate hostility, displeasure or disapproval. In their study they questioned African, African-American and White Americans about their familiarity with the term 'cut eye'. The 'cut eye ' (a hostile look in another's direction) acts as a visual 'put down' and is effective because it violates the 'information preserve' – one of the important 'territories of the self' (the information about self which an individual expects to have full control of whilst in the presence of others) (Goffman, 1972). Rickford and Rickford conclude that:

> A cut-eye provides even more of a 'negative sanction,' since one not only invades but, with the eyes, rummages up, down and about in another's preserve. It's as if the recipient has no power to prevent this visual assault, the very fact that someone else's eyes can run right over him proclaiming his worthlessness (p. 296)

Their study indicates that 94 per cent of African-American informants understood the term 'cut eye' as opposed to 11 per cent of the White American respondents. They also report that their African respondents provided many examples of versions of the term from various African countries such as Kenya and Swahili.

Nobles (1989) also points to the use of eyes by women in the Black community. The 'evil eye' (a steady glare), she argues, focuses attention directly at a person who is not performing as they should. A silent message is sent which communicates dissatisfaction. Its intention, however, is to encourage favourable behaviour and urge the recipients to 'straighten up.'

Byers and Byers (1972) on the other hand, report on the ways in which Black pupils and White in nursery school successfully gain teacher attention by 'catching their eye'. This difference in non-verbal communication indicates that the teacher and pupils did not share similar expectations and an understanding of the meaning of gestures. Four girls, two Black and two White, were observed. One girl from each ethnic group was very active in trying to gain the teacher's attention by looking at her and they concentrated their observations on the 'active' girls. The teacher tried 'to distribute her attentions equally among the children' (p. 23). Their observations of the girls illustrate that the White pupil was successful 57 per cent of the time whilst the Black pupil succeeded in only 11 per cent of her attempts. The White girl, they argue, was able to sense when she could move next to the teacher, sit on her lap, and so on. In contrast, the Black girl's attempts were timed differently: her glances occurred when the teacher's attention was directed away from her and not when the teacher was using 'searching the scene' behaviour, so the teacher did not know when she was trying to gain attention through eye contact. Both the teacher and the Black girl looked towards each other often but 'rarely achieve eye contact and the exchange of expressions that would follow' (p.24).

Deborah Lashley also used her eyes and facial expression to great effect. In the following scenario the children in her class are working independently while she listens to children read. Ross gets out of his seat and goes to where Ms Lashley is seated. He waits for a few moments trying to get his teacher's attention. He fails. Eventually he says

Ross:	Miss [Ms Lashley ignores him for a few seconds and continues listening to another child. She looks up after a short while].
Ms Lashley:	I've given you instructions. I expect you to follow them
Ross:	Miss, shall I write all the words on the board? [Ms Lashley stares at Ross for a short time, her face motionless. She doesn't answer. Instead she asks the other child to continue reading]

Ross is initially ignored and left standing for a short time. Ms Lashley reiterates her position and does not respond to Ross. When he finally asks what he is supposed to do, Ms Lashley gives him a hard look and says nothing. At this point Ross knows he is not going to get an answer, so moves away and returns to his seat.

On another occasion, Mr Thompson is teaching his class division. The children are generally unresponsive but know the topic well. Mr Thompson poses a question to Jacqui, a year six pupil, who is off task attending to her hair. He calls to her:

Mr Thompson:	How many quarter pounds you have in there? [Jacqui looks at Mr Thompson but is unable to answer the question] But is what kind of boo boos we have in this class eh? [He stares at Jacqui, his neck craning towards her] How do you convert 620 into quarter pounds? [His glare is steady and remains focused]
Jacqui:	You divide
Mr Thompson:	What! What! What did you say? [His eyes still firmly fixed on Jacqui]

The use of eyes in this case produced the desired result – the right answer and Jacqui's attention. Mrs Sargeant also uses her eyes as a way of controlling children. Her class are working at their desks when Ysanne gets up from her seat. Mrs Sargeant notices:

Mrs Sargeant:	Ysanne sit down [Mrs Sargeant looks at Ysanne and points towards her seat]
Ysanne:	Miss
Mrs Sargeant:	Sit down [She gets up and stands by Ysanne's chair. All the time she is staring at Ysanne] Where's the pencil? This is no joke you know [Mrs Sargeant remains transfixed. Ysanne sits down and continues with her work]

Ysanne is sent a clear and unmistakable message. Mrs Sergeant's use of eyes is effective in ensuring that she continues with her work.

Eyes and body language

The use of eyes combined with body language was effectively used to control misbehaviour. Mr Wiltshire used such strategies when he wanted to make a point. In his classroom the tapping of the metre stick is often used to caution the children (albeit in a playful way) that they are misbehaving. In the following example, Liam is talking when he is not supposed to. Mr Wiltshire, who has spoken to him about this on several occasions, is becoming annoyed. He gets up from his seat and goes across the classroom to pick up the metre stick. He looks directly at Liam, waves the ruler and says, 'Talk again'. Tevin, who is Black, starts to laugh. Mr Wiltshire turns and stares at Tevin.

The message is clear and unambiguous – continue to talk and I may use the ruler. Mr Wiltshire immediately registers his disapproval to Liam by getting the ruler, waving it and staring directly at him. Tevin is subject to a similar stare. Both Liam and Tevin settle down to work very quickly.

On another occasion, Elaine, a White girl has brought a 'troll' to school. She is sitting playing with it. Mr Wiltshire asks Shawn who is seated next to Elaine a question and notices that she is not paying attention. He looks at Elaine and asks:

Mr Wiltshire:	What did he just say? [He starts to walk towards Elaine's desk, his arms akimbo]
Elaine:	I don't know
Mr Wiltshire:	Well you better pay attention to what's going on here please [He stops and stares directly at Elaine. His face is expressionless. He starts to walk away. Suddenly, he turns on his heels and gives Elaine a long hard look]

Elaine puts the troll down and her full attention is given to the work at hand.

Black pupils indicated during the course of group interviews that they were able to understand the significance not only of their teachers' body language but of the use of eyes. When asked how he responded to discipline Dave, who is Black, reported not only on his feelings, but also on his teacher's behaviour:

He says, 'Sit down boy,' and he keeps on looking at you until you look away, and when you look up again he's still looking at you. It's like he's still telling you off.

Dave, then, has linked his teacher's constant stare with an aspect of control. Kunjufu (1989:50) makes similar observations in a discussion of the use of eyes and tone of voice. He notes, for instance, that an 'assertive teacher' will use strong eye contact, a commanding tone, and will make statements such as: 'I expect you to get back to work. If you do not there will be serious consequences.' Further he argues that:

> This kind of statement and behaviour makes it very clear to the child that the teacher means business...The child and the student are clear about who's in control. This is the assertive model, and it is effective at home as well.

The combination of stance with the use of eyes, therefore, is a powerful communication tool in the Black community.

Paralinguistic features

A practice which is prevalent in many African and Caribbean communities today is that of kissing teeth (also known as sucking teeth) – the lips are pursed and air sucked in through the teeth. It is often used as a way of indicating displeasure, contempt or annoyance. Cruick-shank, writing in 1916, observes:

> A sulking child is told sharply, 'Wha you suck you teeth fo?' ...With eyes lowered and lips pouting, it pictures disgust, discontent-rebellion with the lid on.

Rickford and Rickford (1976: 308) suggest that kissing teeth is an African retention which may survive because it has 'been passed off' with more acceptable 'meanings', such as the effort to remove food from the teeth.' They liken it to a shortened dental click observed amongst the Khoisan and Southern Bantu languages. They also find evidence of teeth sucking in various other African languages such as Mende, Temne, Igbo, Yoruba, Luo, Krio and Cameroon Pidgin. In the Caribbean, the terms 'stchoops' and 'chups' are used to denote kissing teeth. These terms have apparently derived from the convergence of Portuguese *chupar* – meaning 'to suck' and Gambian Krio (Aku) tsipú- to suck teeth – which is adopted from Wolof. Rickford and Rickford conclude that kissing teeth provides 'clear evidence that 'Africanisms' in the New World may reside not only in the exotic, but also in the commonplace' (p.308). Writing about Creole use amongst adolescents in Britain, Hewitt (1986:139) notes that this practice is being adopted by White adolescents in London and reports that it has a 'defiant assertive quality'.

The affective function of kissing teeth is exclamation and its uses are varied. In some cases, it may illustrate disdain for self; in others it may signal irritation at external factors. My observations of kissing teeth in the British context suggest that it occurs habitually amongst many members of the African and Caribbean community, regardless of age or status. It is largely unacceptable, however, for children to kiss their teeth at an adult. Such a transgression may call for instant admonishment and labelling as 'renk' (rude) or 'facety' (barefaced). If, on the other hand, an adult kisses their teeth at a child, it generally occurs as a sign of frustration or annoyance. Kissing teeth is found too amongst same age groupings.

I noted two instances where teachers kissed their teeth at children. In the first scenario Mrs Adesanya is getting increasingly annoyed with Bruno, a Portuguese boy. She has spoken to him several times during the morning and once again she finds that he is not on task.

Mrs Adesanya: Bruno, are you sure there is not something wrong with you? [He does not reply] Bruno, are you sure that there is not something wrong with you?

Bruno: No miss

Mrs Adesanya: Because you behave as if you are sick. Do your work. [Mrs Adesanya then sucks her teeth and walks away]

Although kissing teeth is not part of Portuguese culture, Mrs Adesanya clearly shows her irritation at Bruno's misbehaviour. Judging from his response he understood her meaning perfectly.

In the second scenario, Pearlette Campbell is explaining a mathematical problem to her class. They are seated on the carpet in front of her and are very fidgety. Charles has been asked several times to keep still. Mrs Campbell, however, continues with the task

...eight boys were given six pennies each, how many pennies were there altogether? What's the quickest way to get it? [She notices Charles is fidgeting]. Charles, what are you doing? [She sucks her teeth]

Charles is told clearly and unmistakably way that his teacher is not pleased with him. He is able to recognise the intention of his teacher's behaviour because he shares similar cultural norms. In the case of both Bruno and Charles, the teachers express their annoyance and frustration. Both boys respond by adjusting their behaviour accordingly.

It was pointed out in the discussion in chapter four that kissing teeth is being directed towards White teachers and they are rightly interpreting it as a mark of disrespect. I also found evidence that some Black pupils kiss their teeth at Black teachers. Sheba, a Black girl, reported that she kisses her teeth at her teacher when she is told off. She is obviously aware that it is a form of disrespect but seems unperturbed:

Sheba: Sometimes if she shouts at you, and you talk back at her and suck your teeth, she says, 'Do that to your mother' then sometimes I say, 'What do you mean? I'm not going to do that to my mum. My mum's a respectable woman'.

            [Jaydeen, another student then interjects]

Jaydeen: She says I'm older than your mother...when you are in my class I am your mother

Although Sheba feels justified in being disrespectful to her teacher, she is reluctant to behave in the same way with her mother. It is interesting to note Mrs Adesanya's response, 'Do that to your mother.' Mrs Adesanya clearly equates kissing teeth with disrespect. What she attempts to communicate to Sheba is, 'If you don't kiss you teeth at your mother, then don't do it to me'.

Conclusion

We have seen the ways in which call-response – the principle organising characteristic of African communication – may be used to reinforce group solidarity, share group knowledge and establish rapport. Its highly interactive nature emphasises group participation and a high level of cooperation between teacher and pupils.

Repetition, another feature of Black communications, stimulates pupil involvement and may act as an aid to learning. Proverbial expression and riddling formula, on the other hand, teach children lasting truths and explain complex phenomena in the form of a linguistic puzzle.

Non-verbal communication and paralinguistic features are crucial to an understanding of Black communications. In the context of the school, differences in non-verbal and paralinguistic cues may have far-reaching consequences for both teachers and pupils.

Whilst Black pupils' use of certain features has been identified as a cause of chagrin for White teachers, many Black teachers do, in fact, successfully use non-verbal communication and paralinguistic features as part of their regulatory behaviour. These features are especially effective when used as control mechanisms.

I observed these various aspects of Black communications regularly in classes taught by Black teachers, and how they allowed them to 'culturally connect' with Black children. Not all these behaviours were equally evident among all the teachers. For instance, Mrs Adesanya's use of call-response and repetition were especially pronounced, whilst Mr Wiltshire utilised his skill in many characteristically Black forms of non-verbal communication.

Chapter 6

The three Rs: race, rewards and reprimands

The way in which children acquire the knowledge required for success in school is a complex issue. Children start school with varied social and cultural experiences and differing expectations of the school environment. These differences can have a profound effect not only on their performance in the classroom but also on their relationships with teachers and on their interactions with other children.

The educational system also has expectations of the ways in which children are supposed to perform within the classroom. In short, students are expected to adhere to rules of behaviour and to perform in ways that are acceptable to the teacher and the school. An important point to note, however, is that children are assumed to come to school with some of these behaviours already in place. Schools simply reinforce the 'rules' through codes of conduct.

The recognition of good behaviour in school is generally marked by praise, whilst unacceptable behaviours attract blame. The use of these rewards and sanctions not only enhances teacher/pupil relations but also limits undesirable behaviour. Problems can occur, however, where the cultural values of the teacher and pupil differ. Many studies of teacher interaction in the UK have concentrated on the ways in which minority pupils suffer a disproportionate amount of conflict and criticism (see chapter four). Few studies, however, have considered issues relating to discipline when the teacher and pupils share similar cultural values.

This chapter looks at the strategies used by Black teachers when giving rewards and apportioning blame in the classroom. Based on observations of six Black teachers in two London schools, it starts with an explanation of the purpose of discipline in the school and within the Black family. It then goes on to discuss Black teachers' praising and reprimanding behaviours and illustrates the ways in which Black pupils and White respond to Black teachers' allegedly 'harsh' and 'authoritarian' style. It concludes by discussing pupil perceptions of Black teachers and the implications of Black teacher style for Black children and White.

Discipline in schools

Discipline refers to general beliefs concerning the observance of rules (Alexander, 1973). When this term is used in relation to the school, however, it takes on a range of more specific meanings. For some, discipline is concerned with punishment and dogmatic regimes, whilst for others, it is associated with ideals and principled behaviour. What is clear is that discipline in schools is a contentious issue.

Concepts of discipline

Docking (1987) identifies four reasons why discipline is important to the school: firstly he observes that discipline is a requirement for the social and economic needs of the society; secondly, he argues that it is necessary for the psychological needs of the individual; thirdly, he suggests that it is essential for successful classroom management; and lastly, that it is a prerequisite for educative learning. These various viewpoints will be considered in greater detail below.

You need a disciplined community in order to have a disciplined society

Discipline in the school is often seen to perform an important role in ensuring that children learn to behave in ways that are to the advantage of the society as a whole. In other words, children internalise the behavioural norms and values of the dominant culture and act accordingly. Durkheim (1961) argued that the objectives of a school could be identified by observing the interests of the society. These interests, he claimed, could be described as 'societal facts' – rules, habits, customs and laws which could become internalised through schooling by all members of society. In short, it was to the benefit of society for teachers to cultivate what he called 'the spirit of discipline'. This does not mean that teachers should aim for a uniformity of behaviour, or that they should seek to control children. Rather the ideal is to regularise children's conduct, moderate their egocentric desires and encourage them to respect authority. Durkheim warned teachers, however, of the importance of not allowing their authority to become personalised or repressive. He considered it of paramount importance that the child views the regulations of the school as a reflection of the regulations of the society and not as the expression of the teacher's will.

Bowles and Gintis (1976: 37) add weight to this view. In their work on American schools, they argue that the system of sanctions used was a crucial factor in perpetuating the American capitalist way of life and that:

> Since its inception in the United States, the public school system has been seen as a method of disciplining children in the interests of producing a properly subordinate population.

Children need discipline, it's for their own benefit

This view suggests that the personal needs of the child are as important as the needs of society. Discipline, it is argued, is necessary to promote happiness and emotional security in the child. Durkheim (1961) also recognises that happiness is dependent upon the self-restraint of the individual and argues that this is learned through the experience of external constraint. Ausubel, Novak and Hanesian (1978: 511), too, observe that discipline is important in promoting emotional security:

> Without the guidance provided by unambiguous external controls they tend to feel bewildered and apprehensive. Too great a burden is placed on their own limited capacity for self-control.

An important consideration here, none the less, is that the over-emphasis on discipline can lead parents and teachers to forget that a child's personal adjustment is also dependent upon warmth and affection. In short, it is important to get the balance right.

Effective teaching cannot take place without good discipline

According to this view, a classroom must be orderly if it is to promote effective teaching and learning. In this sense, discipline is closely equated with social control. In fact, the educational literature is full of examples of this kind. The DES (1989: 54), for instance, in a discussion of discipline in schools, is concerned to establish 'what action could be taken ...to secure the orderly atmosphere necessary in schools for effective teaching and learning to take place'. Teachers, too, tend to regard a methodical and orderly environment as important, because they consider a lack of orderliness to be a reflection of their professional competence. Denscombe (1985), for example, observes that teachers are sensitive to noise in the classroom not only because it hampers instruction and learning but also because it may be interpreted as an indication of bad classroom management and ineffective teaching methods.

Given the best will in the world, even a 'natural' teacher cannot ensure that a group of children is going to work together in a harmonious fashion or that the conditions in the classroom are going to be conducive to learning. A certain degree of control is therefore necessary. There is always the danger, however, that concerns about control surpass those about learning. Silberman (1973), for instance, points to the ways in which control can take precedence: learning takes on secondary importance, resulting in what he calls 'schooling for docility'. A major problem with this view, then, is that learning can be sacrificed in the interests of classroom control.

Children need discipline in order to cultivate a disciplined mind

This educative view of discipline claims that 'disciplined' pupils acknowledge that the type of behaviour they are morally obliged to follow is based on beliefs that they think are right. Daunt (1975) points to the relation between discipline and children seeing good reasons for certain actions. The enforcement of rigid school customs such as standing up when a teacher enters the room, he argues, is based on upward rather than mutual respect. As a consequence, such practices are more concerned with encouraging respect for authority instead of instilling a respect for one another. This is not a view shared by everyone concerned with teaching. However, there appears to be more than an element of truth in Daunt's assumption that the kinds of rules enforced and the method of enforcement can help to shape a child's conception of authority.

The notion of discipline is clearly multi-faceted. It may relate to training for society; the application of external constraints; something that teachers do before learning takes place; or the adoption of certain behaviours that the children themselves think are right. Each has its place in schooling. However, it does not automatically follow that a teacher who is successful in one of these areas will be successful in the others – a self-controlled child is not necessarily a disciplined child in the educative sense. Recent concerns about the level of discipline in schools have acknowledged that factors outside of the school can, in fact, influence what occurs within it. The Elton Report, for instance, points out, that teachers are more 'concerned about the cumulative effects of disruption to their lessons caused by relatively trivial but persistent misbehaviour'. It also points to the fact that individual teachers and support staff can make a marked difference to the behaviour of pupils and their eventual educational attainments and pays particular attention to the issue of suspensions and expulsions (DES: 1989).

Given the growing significance of this issue to Black children, it is important to consider the ways in which they conceptualise figures of authority in the home as well as in the school.

Discipline in the Black family

A considerable body of research focuses on the Black family. A major drawback of much of this research is that it has tended to pathologise Black experience, frequently portraying Black mothers as superhuman matriarchs and Black men as unsupportive infidels. Children in Black families are often regarded as the unfortunate recipients of repressive regimes, being frequently chastised without being given any explanation for their alleged misdemeanours.

Early socialisation and child rearing practices

The way in which children develop social attitudes largely depends upon the social world to which they are exposed. The home, the school, the street and the media are all part of this world and the child learns ways of doing things, intentionally or by accident, from other members of the group or from the wider society. Learning the ways of a culture involves not only learning skills but also meanings. Children are then able to construct for themselves a description of the world which includes the events that influence their consciousness. The foundation for these events is primarily laid by parents, as their own construction of the world is embodied in the way they explain things to their children. Older siblings, friends and teachers also complement the parents' structuring of the child's experience. In the case of Black children, however, experiences in the school are sometimes in direct opposition to their lives at home. Black child rearing practices therefore have to be viewed in the context of the basic conflict which exists between the African and the European world view.

The arrival of a new child in the Black family is greeted, as in all cultures, with excitement; the safe passage of children through childhood into adulthood is shaped by their earliest experiences in the home and the school. The ways in which Black families raise their children are often in marked contrast to the Eurocentric ideals of the societies in which they now live. The duality of roles which Black children need to assume is of great significance if one is to comprehend both the complex nature of Black life in the diaspora and Black underachievement in schools.

Lowenthal (1972) observed that, in West Indian family structure, a mother's relationships with her children, especially her sons, is often closer than her relationship with her husband. This, he asserts, is a result of men and women pursuing separate leisure activities. (A similar observation is made by Foner, 1978.) He also points to the fact that child rearing 'is felt to require physical chastisement' and that 'parents frequently resort to the rod' and notes that 'teachers vie with parents as disciplinarians' (p 107). It can be argued, though, that placing undue emphasis on such practices without understanding the underlying reasons, is symptomatic of the deficit tradition and has served to engender negative attitudes towards Black families and their ability to raise their children.

There are, however, studies which offer a positive view. Green (1971), for instance, points to the similarities between the values of women in the Caribbean and West Africa, giving validity to the claim that there is, in fact, a retention of African traditions despite the dispersal of African peoples in the diaspora. Munroe and Munroe (1977) describe the ways in which Kenyan culture encourages cooperation in children, in contrast with American culture which highly values competition. The cultural differences observed between Black communities in Africa and the diaspora point to the importance of studying the Black family within the context of their experiences as peoples who have had to adjust to new situations.

Hale-Benson (1986), writing about the child rearing practices of African American families, argues that the despotism to which Black people have been exposed has made it necessary for the Black family to undertake a very wide range of functions distinct from those found in White families. She identifies, for instance, the preservation and trans-mission of racial heritage; the creation of an alternative frame of reference; a duality of socialisation which requires Black people to perform in ways that are expected of the Black community while also exhibiting the behaviours necessary for economic advancement; the development of self-concept and distinct forms of non-verbal com-munication, physical precocity and movement as important factors in the socialisation process of the child. These considerations, she claims, can have a direct influence on the achievements of Black pupils in schools and can point to ways in which the home, school and com-munity can work together to improve the attainments of Black children.

Heath (1983), in her American study of Trackton, a Black community, and Roadville, a White working class community, found that patterns of language use were closely related to other cultural patterns such as problem solving, group loyalties and patterns of recreation. However their social and linguistic environments differed in a number of ways. In Roadville, for example, verbal interplay was positively valued between children and other members of the community, regardless of age. Children had clearly defined time and physical limits, with family members supervising the objects and events that they should attend to. The role of the parents was critical. Mothers held the major respon-sibility in terms of nurturing and caring for the daily needs of the child, whilst fathers were expected to provide economic support. Children were allowed their own time and space to pursue their own activities, such as reading and playing with toys. Roadville parents believed in the maxim that children need parents. Extended family members and significant others in the community were also responsible for reinforcing the teachings of the parents.

Most children in the Black community of Trackton, however, were raised by their mother and her family. Fathers were expected to 'help out'. Early socialisation was marked by a tendency towards human touch and verbal interactions. Unlike the children in Roadville, there were few time and spatial barriers. Children were generally born into a community and not into the family. Verbal interplay between adults and children was encouraged and the Trackton children soon learned how to 'get the floor'. Parents and other adults considered that they had limited power and that 'the child will be what it is supposed to be'. Boys, in particular, were encouraged to demonstrate to the community their verbal and nonverbal skills, whilst girls performed playsongs, games and role play with older girls. Once children were old enough, they were expected to ask questions, compare items and talk about their feelings, desires and experiences. Without any direct input, they were expected to see things in relation to others and to make sense of the world around them.

The communities held widely different notions about childhood and these influenced decisions about who should teach the child to talk, read and write. In addition, by the time they started school, both Roadville and Trackton children knew how to perform verbally in their respective communities and how to use language to negotiate with significant others in order to achieve their social goals. These opposing methods of child rearing were found to be of particular significance once the children started school. It soon became apparent that even though Roadville children were initially familiar with some of the practices of the school and were relatively successful, by the time they had reached junior high they were failing. For Trackton children, the patterns of failure appeared much earlier and many children left to work in the mills or started families of their own. Of those that remained, many hoped to leave school after achieving a high school diploma.

Praising and blaming

As we have seen, discipline within school and the family is enacted through a complex system of rewards and reprimands, of praise and blame. Writing on the use of praise and blame in oral cultures, Edwards and Sienkewicz (1990) remark that whilst the two behaviours appear at first to be at odds with each other, they do, in fact, operate in similar ways, serving a range of 'social and aesthetic roles' (p. 54).

> In the same way that praise can be used as a social lubricant by emphasising the desirable qualities of the subject, blame plays an important role in maintaining the same social order by persuading or shaming individuals into conformity with community ideals (p. 88).

The importance attached to praise and blame varies from one society to another. In the case of Black children in British schools, such differences may have serious implications for relationships with teachers both Black and White. In chapter four we saw how cultural mismatches have a detrimental effect on the education of Black children, especially boys.

Praise

Black teachers were found to be liberal in their use of praise. A particular feature of this praise is its very public nature. Their words were addressed not only to the child receiving the praise but often to those seated near to them, the whole class or even pupils from other classes. Take Mrs Adesanya and her Year six children at Stockland School. She is circulating in the classroom, monitoring the children's work, when she happens to notice Ian's painting. She shows her approval with great enthusiasm and sincerity and very publicly:

> Oh what a beautiful ...can I see? (to Ian) Children can you look up here please? (to the class). What a careful child, what a very very careful drawing, look at it...he's putting all concentration on this.

The children whose attention has been drawn to Ian's painting respond with gasps and cries of 'Wow'. Nor is this a purely theatrical gesture. Mrs Adesanya follows up her public praise by handing back the painting and standing next to Ian for a little while, watching him work with great interest.

Mrs Adesanya's response to Sid is equally enthusiastic. He is a high achieving pupil who has taken and passed the Common Entrance Exam a year early. He is reading to Mrs Adesanya fluently and with enthusiasm. Mrs Adesanya stops him and declares to the whole class:

> ...Sid has just read to me beautifully, we should be proud of him. He will make a good example of a Stockland pupil when he goes to his new school.

When two girls from a reception class in Haling Park School produced a piece of work which has greatly impressed their teacher, they were sent to share their achievement with Mr Thompson, who teaches Years 5 and 6 and who responds with characteristic enthusiasm:

> Hello, this is what you've done? Oh I tell you. How many of you did this? Yes just you alone? Wow this is good. Wow that's good... that's very very good. Go and show that lady there and then show it to the rest of the class. Which class are you from?

Although Black teachers made wide use of public and enthusiastic praise strategies, there were some differences of opinion as to which kinds of behaviour deserved this response. For example, Mrs Adesanya felt that it was important to praise all aspects of the child.

> It's very very important and gives them that attitude of belonging. It gives them confidence because no child can survive without praise. Even a disruptive child, no matter what little bit they can offer, I keep on reminding them of that positive aspect...no child will survive if you keep on reminding him of the negative attitude.

However, Mr Wiltshire made a distinction between public praise and private encouragement:

> If a child has done some real good work...I think the child deserves to be praised, the one who has not done very well, you will sit down with that child and try to encourage them to work even better.

Such frequent public and enthusiastic praise was used by five of the six teachers in the sample. The one exception was Deborah Lashley, the British born teacher. Take, for instance, an occasion when her class has been working on plurals. Andrew approaches her with his attempt to complete an exercise from the board, on four separate occasions. Each time he is sent back to try again. On the fifth attempt, Andrew gets it right. It is easy to imagine the response which his tenacity would have triggered from most of the Black teachers in the study. However, Mrs Lashley chooses not to share Andrew's success with the rest of the class. Her praise is addressed only to Andrew and is short and to the point: 'Oh thank you!'

One possible explanation for Ms Lashley's apparently different use of praise could be the fact that she was born in Britain, educated within the British system and subsequently trained to teach in a British teacher training institution and that she operates within two cultural frameworks, Black and British. Ms Lashley's use of praise was more similar to that of the White teachers I observed than to her Black colleagues. This was later confirmed in an interview. When asked 'How do you praise the children in your class?', Ms Lashley replied. 'I just tell them, 'Oh that's really good''.

This is not to say that White teachers are ungenerous in their praise. Take, for instance, the case of Mr James, a White teacher of Years 1 and 2 at Haling Park School, who has been listening to pupils read. Rob has made a great effort to read his book without asking for help from Mr James. Mr James congratulates him by saying, 'Very good Rob, I'm impressed, very impressed...I'm going to write some good things about you today. I'm going to write that you had good concentration, that means that you were able to try really hard'.

White teachers would seem to relate more often to children on a one-to-one basis, in contrast with Black teachers, for whom praise is more likely to be a communal event, used to reinforce group values for the class as a whole.

Praise and ethnicity

The qualitative data I collected displayed subtle differences in teacher behaviour, which meant that it was difficult to be sure whether Black children received more or less praise and blame than White children. Biggs and Edwards (1991) report a similar dilemma in their study of teacher-pupil interactions in multi-ethnic classrooms where subtle differences in teacher behaviour remained hidden prior to quantificational analysis.

Teachers' praising and blaming behaviours were therefore analysed over the three days of recording. A total of 127 children were observed; sixty nine Black and fifty eight White. Only children who had been present on each of the three days were included in the analysis. A numerical count was made of occurrences of praise.

As part of this analysis four conditions were observed: private praise, public praise, mild blame and severe blame. Private praise comprised a reward given to children on a one-to-one basis, whilst public praise occurred when a child was rewarded in the presence of others. Mild reprimands characterised a short sanction with no noticeable raise in volume in the teacher's voice. A severe reprimand on the other hand, lasted for more than thirty seconds and was marked by an increase in volume.

A count was made for each child of the number of instances of private praise, public praise, mild reprimands and severe reprimands occurring over the three day period. The data for each variable were then compared in terms of gender, ethnicity and the intersection of gender and ethnicity.

In the first tier of analysis private and public praise were conflated, as were mild and severe reprimands. The data were analysed for gender, ethnicity and the intersection of gender and ethnicity. Statistical computations were conducted using INSTAT, a statistical package suitable for analysis of this kind.

No significant differences in praise were observed during initial analysis ($p=0.2118$). Public and private praise were also analysed separately, but, again, no significant differences were found in the amount of praise directed to Black and White children (private praise: $p=0.052$ (ns), public praise: $p=0.7793$ (ns).

Blame

There were, however, differences in how Black teachers and White handled blame. The reprimanding behaviours of the Black teachers in my study may appear harsher than those of their White colleagues. They occur on a continuum ranging from what I term directness through to shaming and truth telling.

Directness

One of the features which characterised the regulatory behaviour of all the Black teachers in the study was the use of direct instructions. This, in fact, is an aspect of Black socialisation which has attracted some attention in the literature. Baumrind (1972), for instance, in an exploratory study of the effects of parental authority in Black and White preschool children, found that Black parents scored particulary highly on firm reinforcement of rules. She argues that whilst these practices may be interpreted as authoritarian by White standards, they do, in fact, work to the benefit of Black children. Baumrind concludes that Black child rearing practices are more concerned with developing toughness and self-sufficiency and that Black children perceive their parents' behaviours not as rejection but as the actions of caring parents.

Heath (1983) also discusses directness as a feature of Black language and explores the consequences for misunderstanding in the context of the school. In her study of the two American communities she observes that the ways in which teachers asked questions or requested information caused confusion amongst the children from both Trackton and Roadville. Teachers placed great emphasis on modelling polite behaviour and expected the children to respond accordingly. They believed that:

> ... 'good manners' or 'discipline' begins in the years before school, and grave problems... could be alleviated if children learned ...rules for behaving appropriately in the classroom (p. 279).

These patterns of behaviour were rarely stated explicitly in the classroom context, and were based on the cultural expectations of both the teacher and the school. The resulting miscommunication led teachers to suggest that the Black children did not possess normal or mainstream manners and that the White children were losing the manners they came to school with.

For example, the White children from Roadville were able to respond to requests to put items away and showed 'respect' when the teacher was talking. The Trackton children, on the other hand, unused to space function ties (where an activity or event takes place within a particular location), became very bewildered, especially in their first few months at nursery school. As far as they were concerned, no sooner had they started a task than the teacher was asking them to move on to another one. Trackton children also interrupted the teacher during storytime, trying to take the floor, as well as talking freely to their neighbours while the teacher was talking. In sum, the teachers and pupils were at cross purposes; the children were confused and the teachers frustrated. The parents and teachers, however, were united in their intention that the children should learn at school and, as Heath asserts the 'classroom situation... necessitated certain basic rules of cooperation and participation... students had to 'learn school".

The question remained as to how this was to be achieved. Teachers discussed the rules they felt were important for success in school and drew up lists to put in the classroom. Some made videotapes and went into the communities to work alongside parents to illustrate the behaviours they expected at school. What was significant about this process was that teachers, for the first time in their careers, were being forced to state explicitly the patterns of behaviour they expected in the classroom. Some teachers, for instance, in an effort to assist children in time function ties (where an activity was to take place within specified time limits) made large clocks that showed the children when an activity was due to start and when it was to close. Even more significant was the way in which teachers issued directives. Instead of saying 'Can we get ready on time', as an indirect request for children to pack up and get ready for lunch, teachers were forced to be more direct and say 'Put your toys back where you took them from. We have to line up for lunch. Table three will wash hands first' (p.283). Teachers soon became familiar with stating their requests directly and reported that it produced an improvement in the responses they received from the children. However, teachers also used play, story telling and children's programmes to illustrate 'polite ways' of giving orders through the use of hints and indirect requests.

My study revealed many examples of the 'direct' discourse strategies described by Heath. Here is Mr Thompson when he has explained long division to the class. He asks if they understand and they collectively reply, 'Yes'. Kyle, a Black boy, is having difficulty with the topic and turns to his friends for help.

Mr Thompson: Kyle, what's your problem?

Kyle:	I don't understand it sir
Mr Thompson:	What did I ask the class?
Kyle:	If we understood it
Mr Thompson:	Go over there [pointing to a spare table], sit down.

Similarly, in the following extract, Bryan, a Year six pupil in Mrs Adesanya's class who is Black, is painting. Mrs Adesanya sees a dirty paint-brush on the floor, looks at Bryan who is cleaning his brush on the side of the table and says:

If you have finished get up and move out.

Or take the example of Ian, who is White and also taught by Mrs Adesanya. Ian is supposed to be working. Instead he is out of his seat and distracting another pupil.

Mrs Adesanya:	Ian, do you have something to do?
Ian:	Yes Miss
Mrs Adesanya:	Come and show me [Ian does not move] Sit down and do your work. Leave Eric alone.

Directness, then, leaves the addressee in no doubt as to the speaker's intention.

Shaming

Another noteworthy aspect of the Black teachers' interactions with Black children is their use of 'shaming'. The major feature of shaming is the intention of embarrassing the individual. The art of shaming in the Black community is highly developed and a lively part of oral culture. Writers such as Edwards (1979), Labov (1972) and Edwards and Sienkewicz (1990) have pointed to the use of this art form in the UK, USA and the Caribbean. Edwards (1979: 50), for instance, points to the use of shaming routines amongst Black British children in south London. The following, which occurred between two boys, underlines not only the verbal adeptness of the children but also that 'shaming' is a readily understood cultural phenomenon within the Black community.

A: Hush your mouth.

B: Why should I!

A: Cos its closing time.

B: But I ain't a shop! So!

A: I said shut you mouth.

B: Why should I!

A: Cos you lip long like a frog.

B: You don't talk about you own lip do you? You mouth favour the dog.

A: A dog can eat off a frog! So!

B: But a frog can jump over a dog! So! Take a mash don't come flash! Take the shame and don't complain.

The competitive nature of this verbal strategy is clear: each party attempts to outdo the other. The verbal duel is finally won when participant B says 'Take the shame and don't complain'. This sentence has more than a resonance of truth. Shaming draws attention to the individual but is also intended to embarrass.

Shaming is also a strategy used by adults to control children. When Cherylle, a Black girl in Year four, is talking to her friends during a lesson, Mrs Campbell, her teacher says:

> ...Cherylle shut up. All you do is sit and chat, you can't do anything yet you talk all of the time. How are you going to learn if you don't listen? Everybody in the class is more advanced than you. If you want to remain like that, continue.

Cherylle is not only reprimanded but also humiliated in front of the whole class. In short, she is shamed into silence and immediately continues with her work. Similarly, when Trevor, who is also Black, persists in getting out of his seat during a library lesson, Mrs Campbell stares at him and then sighs, 'Oh God'. She stands and watches him for a few moments. When he doesn't respond, she moves over to him and says, 'Oh no'. She then holds him by the hand and remonstrates:

> You make me tired. You had the book just now. Look how many times I've spoken to you.

Truth-telling

Like shaming, the intention of truth-telling is to embarrass the individual. The essential difference is one of degree. The use of 'truth-telling' as a verbal strategy in the Black community has an established history and is a major characteristic of Black parent-child relationships and particularly marked in mother-daughter interactions. Black females are often raised in households where they are the recipients of constant disparaging critiques, frequently justified with remarks such as, 'I would be less than a mother if I didn't tell you the truth'. Audre Lorde's (1982) autobiography of her childhood, *Zami,* provides a glimpse of the strict parenting many Black parents felt necessary when raising their children in often hostile surroundings. The young Audre, not understanding the pervasive nature of racism, decides to run for class president. Feeling excited, she goes home to tell her mother of her plans. She is greeted with the following words:

> What the hell are you doing getting yourself involved with so much foolishness? You don't have better sense in your head than that? What-the-france do you need with election? We sent you to school to work, not to prance about with president-this election-that. Get down the rice, girl, and stop talking your foolishness (p. 61).

When Audre takes part in the election anyway and comes home crying and emotionally battered because she did not win, her mother responds with fury, and strikes her a blow that catches her full on the side of her head. Her mother continues with a verbal beating:

> See, the bird forgets, but the trap doesn't!
>
> I warned you! What you think you doing coming into this house wailing about election? If I told you once I have told you a hundred times, don't chase yourself behind these people, haven't I? What kind of ninny raise up here to think those good-for-nothing White piss-jets would pass over some little jacabat girl to select you anything? (p. 64).

And the beating continues. Lorde was born in the Caribbean, and lived in a northern American city but for many Black people throughout the diaspora, this description has a familiar ring.

Fierce parental critique and the threat of punishment are distinctive characteristics of Black family life and are evidenced in the interactions many Black parents have with their children. The parent-child relationship is one based on the assumption that the parent has the right to rule the child. Truth-telling as described above, therefore, is not just a case of being on the receiving end of a sharp-tongued woman. It also represents a high level of care and concern articulated in what is arguably a negative way. To those unfamiliar with this aspect of Black verbal culture, the seemingly harsh words of a Black mother simply represent an authoritarian stance.

hooks (1993:32), a Black teacher, writer and activist, suggests that although the primary intention of truth-telling may be to assert power over another, it is important to 'distinguish between harsh critiques which may contain 'truth', and liberating truth-telling'. She argues that to be critically analysed and to have aspects of your reality exposed can be a constructive and sometimes pleasurable experience. However, such activities normally take place in a context where the intention is to hurt or wound. Black women in particular, she claims, need to be aware of and re-assess their use of truth-telling in order to check that they are using this often crucial verbal device in an emancipatory rather than destructive way.

Given the obvious significance of this verbal routine, it would be negligent to attempt an analysis of the discourse of Black teachers without considering the cultural meanings attached to the truth-telling interactions that they have with Black children. Take for instance Jadean, who has recently returned from a holiday in Nigeria (she is of Nigerian origin) and is off task and chatting to her friends and distracting others. Mrs Adesanya is sure that Jadean is capable of taking the Common Entrance Exam:

Mrs Adesanya:	Did you go to school when you were in Nigeria? [Mrs Adesanya's arms are akimbo and she is looking directly at Jadean. She has a stern look on her face]
Jadean:	No Miss
Mrs Adesanya:	Your parents should have sent you to school there then you would know how fortunate you are to have these facilities.

To someone not familiar with the way that discipline works in the Black family, this could be perceived as a face threatening and unnecessary reprimand for Jadean. After all, what has her holiday in Nigeria got to do with the fact that she is wasting her time and that of others? When considered in the context of hooks' (1993) observations on truth-telling, however, this interaction is more a reminder to Jadean that if she is to make her way in life she must not squander any opportunity. In a similar scene, Novlette, a Black girl, has finished her work and taken it to her teacher, Mrs Adesanya. It has not been completed to Mrs Adesanya's expectations or to Novlette's usual standard. Mrs Adesanya looks at the book disapprovingly:

> I will not accept. This is a disgrace. Go to your desk and do this again [Novlette returns to her desk].

Black girls may culturally connect with truth-telling strategies. However, Black teachers also use truth-telling strategies with White children. Here for instance the class has been set work on plurals which has been explained to them at great length earlier in the morning. They are supposed to be working at their desks. Ross, a White boy who finds it difficult to concentrate and who craves teacher attention, is standing near to Ms Lashley, who is listening to another student read. She notices him and asks:

Ms Lashley:	Ross can you tell me why you are over here? What did Mr Lewis [the headteacher] say to you this morning?
Ross:	He said about my behaviour
Ms Lashley:	Is that all? Did he say anything about your work?
Ross:	Yes
Ms Lashley:	Your behaviour and your work is the same thing as far as I'm concerned, because if your behaviour was something else your work would be something else. You're not getting any extra treatment from anybody else. They've got to do it, so have you.

Ross:	What have we got to do Miss?
Ms Lashley:	What have we got to do? Why have we been here from 9.40am going through that? Do you think I'm going to teach a class and just because you can't be bothered to sit and listen I'm going to come and speak to you by yourself? It doesn't work that way. I told you before, if you don't want to learn, don't step foot through that door. Isn't that what I told you? [Ross nods] Well then you better go and work out what you've got to do. What have I told you? Go and work it out. You couldn't be bothered to listen
Ross:	But Miss I can't concentrate
Ms Lashley:	Well that's your problem isn't it?

And so the conversation continues. Ross has in one sense been successful in distracting his teacher's attention away from the task at hand. However, Ms Lashley is adamant in her resolve not to give Ross additional help as he has not bothered to pay attention when he should have. Ms Lashley restates her position later in the conversation when she makes it quite clear to Ross that, 'you better find some kind person in this class that's going to explain it to you cause it's not going to be me'.

Although truth-telling is an established part of Black culture and is understood by many Black children its intention may be misinterpreted by White pupils. Thus, what is regarded as an emancipatory critique for some Black children may, in fact, represent a personal assault for White children. What is clear is that, in the same way that Black teachers make explicit to Black children the fact that their race may disadvantage their life chances, they also have to make explicit the purpose and intention of their truth-telling strategies.

Throughout their interactions with Black children, whether in giving instructions, shaming or truth-telling, the most noteworthy feature of Black teachers' regulatory behaviour was its directness. White teachers, in contrast, tended to take a more indirect approach. For instance Asoumi, a pupil of Arab origin, is not in his seat and is distracting other pupils, Mr James sees him and says, 'Asoumi'. There is no response and once again, Mr James repeats, 'Asoumi'. Asoumi looks around and Mr

James continues, 'Sit down'. This whole exchange is respectful of the fact that Asoumi is being reprimanded in front of the class. In fact, when Mr James says 'Sit down', there is a noticeable reduction in the volume of his voice. The intention here appears to be to register disapproval whilst not drawing too much attention to the original misdemeanour, thus reducing the possibility of a face threatening situation for the child.

Blame/reprimands and ethnicity

Although there were no significant differences between the praise offered by Black teachers to Black children and White, it was important to consider whether there were differences in the distribution of blame.

Blame was divided into two categories: mild and severe. A mild reprimand comprised a short sanction with the teacher's voice not noticeably raised. A severe reprimand lasted for more than thirty seconds and was marked by the teacher's voice becoming louder.

In the first level of analysis mild and severe reprimands were conflated. The results of combined mild and severe reprimands then, are highly significant (0.0). Moreover, they demonstrate that Black children receive significantly more reprimands than White children.

In the second tier of analysis, mild and severe reprimands were treated separately. In both cases, significantly more reprimands were directed towards Black children than White (mild reprimands, $p=0.0162$, severe reprimands $p= 0.0$).

It is possible to offer two separate but complementary explanations for these patterns. First, Black teachers may realise, whether consciously or unconsciously, that Black children and White are socialised in different ways and that White children may misinterpret some aspects of their teaching style. Second, they are aware that Black children are very familiar with their control strategies and will therefore 'culturally connect'. Leroy Wiltshire of Haling Park School observed that:

> My relationship with Black children is more relaxed in that because of the West Indian background you have a full knowledge of how parents might tend to respond. Based on that you know how far you can go with the Black child. Whereas with the White child one is always sort of on the defensive. So that, for me personally, the

relationship I have with the Black child is different to that with the White child. It's more of a camaraderie with the Black child. Because this relationship is not extended to the White child, the White child is not as close to me. It's a more formal situation. Where I tend to make a joke out of an incident with a Black child, I'm very careful not to do that with the White child.

Possible explanations

As we saw in chapter four, studies which have concentrated on the role of the Black teacher have tended to portray them as strong disciplinarians and upholders of the *status quo*. However, more recent work focusing on effective teachers of Black students indicates that, contrary to the findings of earlier studies, Black teachers display a range of cultural patterns which may influence what they teach, why they teach it and how it is taught. More importantly, these teachers exhibit patterns of behaviour which are closely related to their identification with, knowledge of, or membership of the Black community.

'Connectedness'

Writers concerned with the effectiveness of teachers of ethnic minority students in America have pointed to 'connectedness', that is, the influence of the family and community on the teachers themselves, and on the students they teach. Michele Foster (1991) for example, asserts that connectedness is characterised by two important features: the quality and depth of the relationship the teacher has with their pupils and the mutual trust which exists between the teacher and the parents. These teachers stress the interrelationship between the family, the community and the church. In their teaching they adopt a 'parenting stance'. So they are not only concerned about matters of discipline but also see their role as 'guiding' the children in their care. Kin-like relationships are also a feature of connectedness, and many of the female teachers in Foster's study reported that when the children are in their care they regard themselves as their 'mothers'. In conclusion, Foster asserts that connectedness is a critical component of responsible teaching and points to other Black scholars who have identified this theme as part of their work on Black family life (Hill, 1972; Stack, 1974) .

Connectedness in British classrooms

'Connectedness' was evident in my study in a number of ways. Many teachers pointed to their personal experience of schooling and highlighted the ways in which it has shaped their practice in British schools. Another important factor which emerged from the data was the relationship between home and school. The absence of good home-school communication often led to misunderstanding and increased the chances of failure for Black children. Evadne Sargeant, talking about her choice of teaching as a career, points to the lasting impressions that her own teachers made upon her, and the persistence of one headteacher who ensured that she pursued the career of her choice.

> I come from a family of teachers. I always wanted to be a teacher and if I should live my life again I would want to be a teacher... I had very good teachers. They were not just teachers in that they were there to teach. They looked after you, they wanted to help you... I remember my old headteacher. I told her I wanted to be a teacher but my aunt who I was living with wanted me to be a seamstress. My headteacher came to the house because she got me a scholarship... That was the type of thing that teachers do. They not only saw you as their pupils but beyond that they looked at your future.

Embedded within Evadne's description is a conception of the teacher's role which encompasses cognitive, social and emotional growth. It also illustrates the interrelationships that existed between the school, the family and the community. This view was reinforced by Pearlette Campbell, who spoke about the inspiration she gained from watching her teachers and the satisfaction that teaching gives her now:

> I looked at my teachers and saw how they treated me and other students in the classroom. I wasn't aware of their frustrations, but I was aware of the joy and happiness. They would come and hug you when you do their task efficiently... Teaching was a very enjoyable thing... it still is.

These early educational experiences, it appears, have had a lasting effect on who these teachers are today, why they are teaching and how they go about educating other people's children.

Connectedness was also shown in the close personal relationships that exist between the teachers, their pupils and the children's parents. Adebola Adesanya, for example, reports on the similarities she finds between her roles as a mother and teacher:

> If I am to discuss my role as a teacher it is very difficult. I can't divorce my role as a teacher from my role as a mother. It's still a continuity... Some children make the mistake and call me 'mummy', because when they come through my door I tell them 'Trust me, regard me as your mother'.

Winston Thompson also considered it important to establish and maintain a good relationship between the pupil, the home and the school.

> I do a lot of home visits because I know it's the basis of a good education. Know the child to be educated. You cannot educate a child unless you know him. You must know his background, his environment and how his parents are guiding him.

In his teaching Mr Thompson regularly reminds Black children of their ethnicity, saying 'remember you're Black'. Later in the interview he pointed to the way in which aspects of his discourse with Black children is a matter of concern amongst his White colleagues and has caused some of them to view his practices as unorthodox.

> I hit them hard [the pupils], knock them down and try to build them back up again. When they realise you are building them up again, they will come and say 'remember you're Black'. This is a good feeling because you can see that they are realising. They respond in a positive way. The White teachers get very nervous when I say things like that. The headteacher's opinion is that he does not mind as long as it does not come back to the school, or the teacher.

It is normal then for teachers to work alongside children and their parents as an extended family member in many parts of the Caribbean and Africa. Although there has been a growing emphasis in British education on the importance of partnership with parents (eg Edwards and Redfern, 1992; Kenway, 1994), this is an area in which much work remains to be done. Teachers in the present study, including Winston Thompson, specifically referred, for instance, to the fact that few of their White colleagues considered the wider community in the same way as they did. For, whilst many teachers try to work in partnership with parents, it does not necessarily follow that they regard their relationship as an extension of the family or that they identify with the community.

Significant adults

The school, teachers, parents and significant others all play an important part in the Black child's understanding of their social world and their place within it. The difficulties faced by Black children in school are further compounded by the inter-relationships between the home and school, and in their interpretation of the events surrounding them. A crucial factor in this understanding is how they perceive and respond to figures of authority, especially within the context of the school.

A study which has attempted to answer this question was conducted by Henderson and Washington (1975). They observe the process of social control within a Black American community and contrast it with an elementary school. Henderson and Washington argue that adults in the Black community play an important role as agents of social control. A network of significant others correct undesirable behaviour and notify parents when it happens. The crucial point about this control system, however, is that it operates externally to the child, so the child is conscious of an external locus of control. In schools, however, teachers and other adults frequently expect children to behave as though they have internalised the rules of social control. As a consequence, they do not function in ways that are consistent with Black children's expectations of how adults should relate to them in situations that require the enforcement of social controls.

Henderson and Washington conclude that Black children's perceived misbehaviour in school can be described in two ways. Firstly, children realise that adults in school do not function in the same way as adults in the home/community and that only extreme acts of misbehaviour are reported, as adults in school are not community agents of social control. Secondly, there is a general belief that children come to school having already internalised social control. Teachers expect Black children to behave like their White counterparts. However, in many cases, teachers and pupils have mutually incompatible expectations of one another, some of which are resolved whilst others remain problematic.

Differing perceptions of schooling by teachers and pupils can in some instances lead to a mis-match in expectations. For Black children this is further complicated by cultural expectations which vary from those of mainstream society. A major consequence is that Black children's performance in school is sometimes misinterpreted by teachers unfamiliar with Black children or their families.

Black teachers in the present study were observed commenting on behaviours which, in themselves, had little to do with the school but were in fact based on the personal expectations of the teacher as an adult. Mrs Sargeant, a Year One and Two teacher at Stockland School, for example, noticed that Devante, a Black boy, had worn to school an eye-catching yellow shirt which exposed his chest and back. Devante is caught talking when he should be listening. Mrs Sargeant not only comments on his inattention but also registers her disapproval of his dress sense in a very public way in front of the whole class:

> Just keep yourself quiet. Do you see me come to class and sit down like that in front of you? Well don't do it in front of me. You put on your clothes. [Devante puts on his coat] Next thing you'll be coming here naked.

Not only is Devante reprimanded for talking but Mrs Sargeant uses this as an opportunity to inform the class of her expectations regarding acceptable school dress. Later that day another pupil is giving a presentation to the class and Devante, who has obviously forgotten about the earlier incident, is sitting with his coat off. Mrs Sargeant restates her position:

Mrs Sargeant:	Turn around Sir. Take off that shirt, put on your thing. [She points to Devante's coat] You come back in here with it again? Take your coat go outside and change and come back. Come on.
Devante:	I'll put my coat on
Mrs Sargeant:	No go outside. I shall talk with your mother because she didn't know you wore that to school this morning [Devante leaves the classroom]

Mrs Sargeant again registers her disapproval of Devante's attire. More importantly, this time Mrs Sargeant adds that she is going to contact Devante's mother, as she believes that his mother does not know that he has come to school dressed this way. The use of 'parent as threat' is a feature of Black culture and is used as a way of instilling discipline. Mrs Sargeant, it could be argued, is acting as a 'significant adult', assuming a role which would be unusual in mainstream British society. The fact that Devante complies with Mrs Sargeant's request to leave the classroom and returns later with his shirt off shows that he understands the purpose of the reprimand – and at the end of the school day, he asks Mrs Sargeant not to contact his mother.

Or take the example of Tevin, a year five pupil taught by Mr Wiltshire, when he makes a minor error whilst attempting a maths problem. Tevin completes his task and stands up to let Mr Wiltshire know that he has finished:

Tevin:	Sir sir [Mr Wiltshire goes to Tevin's desk to mark the work]
Mr Wiltshire:	What we dealing with here? What the sign say?
Tevin:	Pounds sir
Mr Wiltshire:	Pounds...what is this here?
Tevin	[realising he has made an error]: Oh pounds
Mr Wiltshire:	Hold on, hold on ...what we dealing with here?
Tevin:	Pounds
Mr Wiltshire:	Money ...where is the sign? [Mr Wiltshire stares at Tevin and simultaneously raises his hand as if to hit him]
Mr Wiltshire:	A little tick. You can't get no fancy tick for that
Tevin:	Thank you sir

Tevin has, on the face of it, committed a very small error by not inserting the correct mathematical notation. He eventually realises his mistake and corrects it. Mr Wiltshire's response, however, is to continue to draw attention to Tevin's error by repeating the question twice more.

Finally, although he marks the work as correct, he advises Tevin that 'you can't get no fancy tick for that'. Later Mr Wiltshire reported that his response was influenced by Tevin's character but he does concede that his response to Tevin is 'different' to that of other pupils in the class:

> I'm not sure that I would have responded to another child in the same way. Tevin is a special case. Perhaps I deal with Tevin in a different way to others in the class.

Mr Wiltshire is clearly marking the boundaries of what is an acceptable standard of work and is making it clear that he will accept nothing less.

Whilst it can be argued that Mr Wiltshire may feel that his actions are permissible in his role as a significant adult in the Black community, it is not acceptable as part of his professional duties as a teacher in a British school. Further, if Mr Wiltshire had behaved similarly towards a White pupil, his actions might not have been interpreted in the same way.

Yet another example involves Nzinga, a Black pupil taught by Mr Thompson. When she is discovered playing with a calculator she is made the object of an embarrassing exchange.

Mr Thompson:	So now we've got our statement what is the next thing we do? Sixth year come on. Nzinga stand up and tell me what is the next thing we do. Come on Nzinga, come and show me come [she moves towards the board] Come on girl, move man, sitting down there playing with calculator [She is given the chalk] Show me what is the next stage we'd take, you've got your statement written out [Nzinga stares at the board] Come on you don't know?
Nzinga:	No
Mr Thompson:	Because you weren't listening. Now stand right there please. Move out of the way and pay attention.

Nzinga is left standing at the front of the class looking shamefaced. She is also subjected to a public form of cussing:'Come on girl, move man... sitting down there playing with calculator'. The comment occurs almost as an aside that has been verbalised for the benefit of the class. In short, the teacher's intention here was to alert Nzinga that he was not going to accept inattentiveness from her and that he would draw attention to her in front of the class, if necessary. Further, he wanted her to recognise that she couldn't afford to be wasteful of her limited time in school and should, therefore, concentrate fully at all times. Later Mr Thompson explained that his response to Nzinga was based on his expectation that she would be familiar with the work and therefore able to answer the question.

Nzinga, of course, is very bright and should have been concentrating on the work. But obviously she was not there, she was somewhere else. She wasn't listening and I was showing her up to the class. Not only was I trying to show her up but also to cut her down to size.

Even though Mr Thompson does not point directly to the differential treatment of Nzinga on the grounds of her ethnicity in this example, my observations of his classroom practice and his comments on page 120 indicate that, he does, in fact, treat Black pupils differently from White.

Contrast these episodes with the treatment which Helen, a Black girl, receives from Ms Brown. Over a period of time, I had noticed that Helen, a Black girl in Year four at Haling Park School, was excessively attention-seeking. Her behaviour had always struck me as bizarre. Dancing and singing around the room and putting stickers all over her face are just two incidents I witnessed. Ms Brown explained that she did not get much attention at home and so craved attention at school. One day, after the class had been sewing, an activity that Helen obviously enjoyed and wanted to continue, I witnessed this incident:

Ms Brown: Yes, what is it?

Helen: This [She points to her Maths book]

Ms Brown: So write in the answer 5 x 3 equals...You know I think you're asking me silly questions this morning

Helen	[starts to whine] I don't like it
Ms Brown:	You just don't want to do it do you?
Helen:	I'll do it later, I'll do my sewing
Ms Brown:	No, it's the dreaded sewing isn't it? [Helen then sits on the teacher's lap and starts to bounce up and down as if she were riding a horse] Well as soon as you do that, you can get on to your sewing [Helen throws her book on the table]. I'm not going to let you do your sewing first. I'm not going to let you do that. Take your hand off [The teacher half eases and half pushes Helen off of her lap] I'm not going to let you do that. Sorry [She turns away and starts to talk to another pupil, Helen lingers then eventually goes back to her table. She is not working. A few moments later the teacher notices]
Ms Brown:	Helen just sit down and get on.

Helen's behaviour is clearly unacceptable. She monopolises the teacher's time and ensures that she cannot do anything else by sitting on her. Yet the teacher is willing to negotiate with her and even apologises for giving her work. The fact that the teacher associates Helen's misbehaviour with a lack of attention at home is indeed worrying, not only because it causes problems for Helen, her classmates and her teacher but, more importantly, because Helen's 'difficulties' are being linked with a deficit in her home life. While it may be true that Helen does not receive attention at home, if one considers the example above in the context of Henderson and Washington's (1975) findings that Black children expect adults to behave in particular ways where boundaries are clearly marked, it would also be possible to argue that the teacher is not meeting Helen's expectation of adult behaviour. The teacher has allowed this type of behaviour to become an established pattern. In fact, it can be argued that the teacher's reluctance to exercise her authority in class is partly responsible for the scenario above. Equally pertinent, the teacher has not considered the extent to which her own behaviour affects the behaviour of the children in her class.

Teacher interactions with Black and White children

Studies of teacher-pupil interaction have tended to focus exclusively on minority pupils' relationships with White teachers. In the UK writers such as Wright (1986; 1992), Gillborn (1988; 1990b), Biggs and Edwards (1991) and Sewell (1997) have commented upon the ways in which a child's ethnicity can influence their interactions with teachers and their experiences of teacher expectations. Very little attention has been paid to the interactions between ethnic minority pupils and ethnic minority teachers.

My study confirms the findings of previous research that Black pupils tend to be treated more critically than their White peers. The essential difference, however, would seem to be that Black teachers are behaving within a cultural framework where the firm reinforcement of rules is related to their desire for Black children to achieve their full potential. In short, Black teachers' critical discourses with Black children, although couched in what can be construed as negative language, may have as their explicit objective the development of toughness and self-sufficiency. Further, this may be perceived by some Black children, although not necessarily all, as nurturant care taking.

My study found that Black teachers reprimanded Black children significantly more often than White children. This should not be taken as showing that Black children's behaviour is in any way more problematic than that of their White peers. Rather, many Black teachers may feel that they have to be more 'critical' of Black children to ensure that they perform to their highest standard, achieve academically and ultimately succeed in their chosen lifestyle. This type of 'hidden curriculum' has also been reported by Lightfoot (1973). In a study of two Black teachers in a predominantly Black American schools, she observed that despite the differing educational philosophies and practices of the teachers, both were committed to providing an education that enhanced Black children's attainments and ultimately gave them greater control over their destiny. The teachers' conscious attempts to prepare children for an unjust society meant that their communications had an underlying political meaning. Lightfoot concludes that:

> In the hearts and minds of these two teachers, educational goals were closely related to their conception of the political process outside the classroom. (p. 240-41)

My observations of Black teachers support this position and suggest that Black teachers were particularly sensitive to the misbehaviour of Black pupils, taking extra steps to curtail it as and when it arose. Mr Thompson, a teacher at Haling Park, reported that:

> When the Black ones play around I tell them in front of their peers, 'When you want a job, John who is White will get the job. Just like that. But you have a disability from the start, you are Black. Whatever you do has to be ten times better than John for you to survive'. I am here to help Black and White but I am keeping an eye out for the Black one... In fact, when I look at the Black ones and they're playing about I shout at them louder. I tell them you are letting me down.

Similar observations are made by Cazden (1988), who, in her study of patterns of language use in American classrooms, observes that where teachers belong to the same reference group as the children they teach, their sense of cultural solidarity may display itself in two ways. Firstly, it can be implicit and unspoken; secondly, it may be explicit and continually reinforced in classroom interaction.

Take this scenario from my study. Dave, who is Black, has not taken care with the presentation of his work. He notices that Mr Thompson is moving about the class looking at individual books and quickly turns to a new page. Mr Thompson notices this and looks at Dave in a questioning way:

Dave:	I'm starting again
Mr Thompson:	What?
Dave:	It's untidy sir
Mr Thompson:	Well you should not have produced work for me that was untidy. Come on, let me see it.
	[He leafs through the book] So what's all this incomplete fraction there man? So what have you done this morning? Apart from wasting your book? Dave, what is this you've done in your book? What is all

> this skipping of pages and wasting all the
> book for? Dave, you are going to clean up
> this book and work in it for the next year.

Other teachers also reported that they tended to be harder on Black than on White pupils. Leroy Wiltshire related this to his Caribbean origins and the position of Black people in British society.

> My response has to do with my upbringing and perhaps this is different because I was born in the Caribbean. I tend to be a little bit hard with the Black ones because I feel this is a White society and what the Whites can do and get away with, the Blacks cannot do and get away with. I feel my job is much more than teaching decimals and fractions – it is instilling values. One of the values that has to be instilled in them is that you have to work harder than the White. This is the reality, so I tend to be a little more hard with the Blacks than with the Whites.

Responses of Black pupils

It was evident that many pupils, Black and White, were conscious that Black teachers behaved differently to White teachers, highlighting features which they felt important.

Black teachers' use of blaming strategies arguably carry particular cultural significance for many Black children who are acutely aware of the 'hidden' meanings in their teachers' discourses. Some Black children in the study were clear that their teachers wanted them to achieve far above the 'average'. Olu, who is taught by Deborah Lashley, reported that his teacher often advised him not to step a foot in her classroom unless he was going there to learn. When asked if he liked having a Black teacher, Olu replied:

> Yes I do like having a Black teacher because she wants nothing but the best.

This implicit knowledge can increase motivation, improve attitudes and enhance the learning process. Other Black pupils reported that they preferred Black teachers because they thought that they were able to 'control' the class. Nzinga, a Year six Black pupil of Mr Thompson at Haling Park reports:

...he's much stricter, he gives you harder work and he teaches you better and if you get to go in his class I think you're lucky...cause he teaches you better than the other teachers.

Similarly, Rosalind, a pupil in Mr Wiltshire's class asserts:

...most Black teachers are strict and if the class goes wrong they can put it back. I just think they're better.

Carolyn, a Black year six pupil in Mr Thompson's class, culturally connects with her teacher's behaviour which she relates to her perception of teachers in the Caribbean:

...he's different from all the other teachers...like he says he's going to hit you. In Jamaica if you do anything like talk you get beaten with the cane or the ruler. I find it different to some of the White teachers. Like Nzinga said, some of the White teachers are soft.

The subject of Black teachers as role models also emerged. Here is Marcus, in Year three at Haling Park School, who has only been taught by White teachers:

...I've never had a Black teacher...I would like to have a Black teacher for seven years because all of my teachers have been White. I've never had a Black teacher. All I want to have is a Black teacher.

Similarly, Julian a pupil in Mr Thompson's class, remarks:

It's like a role model because most times you see White teachers in the class... throughout my whole school life, Mr Thompson is the first Black teacher I've had.

Although many Black pupils value the experience of being taught by Black teachers, not all prefer to be taught by them. Aleisha in Year four said 'I don't like them', and Sinieta replied 'No' when asked 'Do you like having a Black teacher?' They do, however, perceive Black teachers as possessing qualities which they do not recognise in White teachers.

Responses by White pupils

The White children I observed, although recognising the differences between Black and White teachers' style, appeared to adapt to the behaviours of Black teachers without any difficulties. For instance Toya, a White girl in Year Six, felt that the race of the teacher was unimportant:

I don't think it has anything to do with what race they are, because Mr Wiltshire is just a funny man. He likes to joke about. It's how they sort of react to children.

In constrast Alan, a pupil from Haling Park taught by Mrs Campbell, felt that differences did exist between Black teachers and White. He believed that Black teachers gave 'harder' work, and expressed his feelings thus:

Alan: We have different classes and some people are Black like Mrs Campbell and some teachers are White

CC: Right. Do you think that makes a difference?

Alan: Yes

CC: What sort of difference?

Alan: Some teachers are Black and some are White

CC: Yes, but what's that got to do with it? Don't they teach the same way? Are you saying that the Black teachers here are different to the White teachers?

Alan: No

CC: Saying that is fine. It's OK to say that.

Alan initially confirmed that he felt that there might be differences between Black teachers and White. However, his subsequent denial may well have been a defensive reaction to being questioned by a Black interviewer. When he was, in a sense, given permission to pursue this line of thought, he finally confirmed his view that there were differences. The interview continued cautiously:

Alan: They don't teach the same way, like they give harder work.

Conclusion
Discipline within the school and the Black family follows distinct and observable patterns. In both environments a complex system of rewards and reprimands, of praise and blame, is established. Descriptions of the Black family often refer to their traditional and authoritarian stance; these observations have also been applied to the practice of Black

educators. When such observations are viewed within a broader cultural framework, however, the emancipatory nature of Black reward and reprimanding strategies becomes clearer.

In the context of the school, praise and blame strategies have important implications for teacher-pupil relationships. Black teachers not only offer praise in a very public way but they also display a range of reprimanding behaviours characterised by directness. We have also seen that they give all children similar amounts of praise, but give Black children significantly more blame.

Possible explanations for this phenomenon include the connectedness that exists between Black teachers, Black pupils and their parents; and the way in which Black teachers perform the role of significant adult, commenting upon behaviours which are normally regarded as being outside the realms of the school.

Ultimately, for many pupils in schools their first interactions with teachers require a period of re-adjustment. For some Black children their experiences of being taught by Black teachers may signal the start of a learning process which goes beyond the narrow confines of the classroom. Furthermore, some Black children may identify with aspects of their teacher's practice and regard these actions as nurturant caretaking. This is not to suggest, of course, that all Black children react in the same way. The children's comments illustrate that not all Black children like being taught by Black teachers.

The implications of Black teaching style for White pupils are less clear. No White pupils made negative reports to me about Black teachers. My own ethnicity, however, could have influenced their responses. It should also be noted that although many White pupils may recognise some aspects of Black teaching style, they may not be familiar with all. There is a possibility of cross cultural miscommunication.

Chapter 7

The intersection of gender and ethnicity in teacher-pupil relationships

The gender roles of men and women in the Black community, as in any other community, are highly significant, in discussions of socialisation patterns and also education. This chapter starts with a discussion of the relationship between language, gender and education, and the ways in which classroom talk displays patterns of male dominance. It then goes on to discuss the differing ways in which Black girls and boys have been portrayed in the educational literature and explores the effects of these assessments on Black children's educational outcomes. The results of a quantitative analysis of praise and blame across four dyads – Black boys and White boys, Black girls and White girls, Black boys and Black girls, and White boys and White girls indicate the possible interactions of gender and ethnicity.

Language and gender

Many studies have pointed to the ways in which gender-influenced behaviour is mediated through language and highlight their effects on the language socialisation of children. Gleason (1973) for instance, contends that language use with children is related to gender in terms of both the target and source of the message. Variation has been observed in politeness routines used with girls as opposed to those used with boys (Corson, 1993). There is also a tendency for fathers to interrupt their children more than mothers, especially in the case of girls, thus producing a fixed pattern of language behaviour very early in a child's life. Adults thus appear to establish social conventions for language use quite early in children's lives and use language as the medium for achieving this. As Philips, Steele and Tanz (1987) observe:

> Parents speak differently from each other; they speak differently to boys and girls; and boys and girls speak differently (p. 124).

Corson (1993:124) argues that when children start formal education, they arrive with 'robust patterns of linguistic socialisation that are already well established in infancy and early childhood'. The school arguably goes on to reinforce gender-biased practices by maintaining patterns of language use that have become second nature. It is to a discussion of these issues that we now turn.

Gender issues in classroom interaction

The differential treatment of girls and boys in mixed-sex classrooms has been studied extensively in the research literature (see for example Mahoney, 1983; Swann and Graddol, 1989). These studies indicate that girls are marginalised in the education process in a number of ways, including the active efforts of boys to 'put them in their place', and male 'control' of the classroom and the school which indirectly poses a threat to the 'authority' of female teachers.

In their study of American classrooms, Sadker and Sadker (1985) observed that talk in the classroom was mainly a male dominated activity. Boys spoke three times as often as girls and were eight times more likely to call out the answers to questions. For their part, teachers, were more likely to accept boys' answers, even though they had called out. Girls, on the other hand, were reprimanded for adopting similar behaviours. Evidence to support this view is found in British research conducted by French and French (1984; 1994) in primary classrooms. They report that talkative boys often use specific strategies in order to gain increased classroom talk. By answering the teachers' questions in an unusual way, they are able to gain extra turns in classroom conversation.

Awareness of these patterns has led some researchers to try consciously to address the imbalance. Spender (1982) for example, argues that it is virtually impossible to divide one's time equally between boys and girls but Whyte (1986) in a study of 'Girls into Science and Technology' finds evidence to the contrary. She argues that the encouragement of equal participation creates a situation whereby teachers can divide their attention equally between boys and girls. However, she also reports that a head of Science involved in the study who had successfully established an atmosphere of equal participation, felt as if he had devoted ninety per cent of his attention to the girls!

Writing on male dominance in the classroom, Swann (1988) argues that not only is talk mediated through or controlled by the teacher but also that, if boys are allowed to dominate classroom discourse, it is often with the tacit agreement and/or acceptance of the teacher. In a study of primary school classrooms, Swann notes that teachers' verbal and non-verbal behaviour may send signals that work to the benefit of boys and the detriment of girls. Reporting on her observations of two teachers, she finds that, regardless of individual teacher style, classroom interaction tends to favour boys. In one classroom, the teacher positioned herself so that she could see the boys more clearly than the girls. Additionally, girls were helped to use equipment whilst boys were given instructions on how to use it. Swann also reports that boys in this classroom contributed more talk in terms of number of turns taken and amount of words used. Boys were thus able to 'control' classroom talk. When the teacher selected pupils to speak, she often chose girls. The general pattern in the class, however, was that pupils would often 'chip in' – with the result that boys were again at an advantage, responding twice as often as girls. Another aspect of teacher behaviour which favoured boys was their use of gaze. This teacher looked towards the girls forty per cent of the time and at boys sixty per cent of the time.

In the other classroom, similar findings emerged. The teacher had a different style and although interaction was lively, classroom business was kept under teacher control. Pupils in classroom B tended to raise their hands instead of calling out, yet Swann observed that boys, on average, got more turns, the teacher tending to respond to the child who put their hand up first. These pupils were usually boys who not only raised their hands first but did so more decisively and subsequently got to answer more teacher questions. The girls who raised their hands usually did so only after the teacher had already selected someone to speak. This teacher's gaze behaviour showed that she concentrated 65 per cent of her attention on boys and 35 per cent on girls. When she posed a question to boys, her gaze often stayed with them. However, on the few occasions where her gaze was focused on girls, she averted her gaze mid-way or even throughout the interaction. Swann concludes that:

> This overall pattern of gaze behaviour may give boys generally more positive feedback and encourage them to respond to questions when they came (p. 137).

In sum, boys, through established patterns of gender specific language behaviour, are given more opportunities than girls to take control of the floor in classroom discourse. Further, these behaviours are often validated by their teachers.

Inasmuch as these observations are true of all children, interactions involving Black children might be similarly influenced by ethnicity.

The portrayal of Black pupils

The prevalent notions held about Black children in school relate to underachievement. This stereotypical view fails to highlight the successes of many Black students and rarely recognises the improvements in Black children's attainments over the past ten years or so (Hymas and Thomas, 1994). There is also a tendency to stereotype Black girls and boys in rather different ways: some teachers tend to regard Black girls as 'loud' and 'difficult to manage' (Evans, 1988; Mirza, 1992) and Black boys as 'surly' and 'aggressive' (Gillborn, 1988; Wright, 1992).

Research on Black girls

In a study of Black girls in a London secondary school, Fuller (1980) considers that Black girls formed 'school-based sub-cultures'. These subcultures are based on the girls' strong identification with the Black community and their roles as young women within it. Whilst the girls displayed a commitment to education and academic success, their behaviour at school showed signs of ambivalence. To be identified as a good pupil meant that they exposed their ambitions for further study and future job prospects. They felt that such exposure would attract unwarranted and unwanted attention from their female peers and, more importantly, Black boys. Additionally, the girls associated being good with being boring, immature and not knowing how to have fun. In classroom interactions with teachers, they felt that 'bright' pupils put too much faith in teachers' opinions of their capabilities. As far as they were concerned, public examinations would be marked by outsiders so the teacher's view was not a matter for great concern. Fuller concludes that 'it seems reasonable to suppose that, in coming to a sense of their own worth, the girls had learnt to rely on their own rather than others' opinion of them' (p. 61). Fuller also points to the 'resentment' caused by the over burdening of domestic tasks on Black girls. Whereas the girls were expected to wash-up and childmind etc, boys did not assist in these chores to the same degree, nor was there an expectation that they would do so.

Writing about her experiences of teaching in London, Evans (1988), a Black American, points to the ways in which 'those loud Black girls' (a euphemism for the perceived misbehaviours of Black girls) in her former school exasperated her mainly White colleagues. The girls' use of Patois and their refusal to 'conform' to school rules was a source of frustration for many teachers. She observes that Black girls come very close to the realms of 'bad behaviour' without actually breaking any formal school rules.

Evans herself made rather different decisions in her own career as a student:

> I was not loud myself; I was one of the quiet, almost to the point of silent, Black or 'coloured' girls who did her homework, worked hard, seldom spoke unless spoken to and was usually to be found standing on the margin of activities. I demanded no attention and got none (p. 184).

She also comments on the cost of academic success on the personal, social and psychological development of the individual and on their families.

> The prize of a good education was attained at the cost of great sacrifice on the part of one's parents, sometimes the entire family. Aside from this cost, another price is paid by the recipient of an education, and this is the personal cost of de-culturalisation, or de-Africanisation, whereby all personal expressions of one's original African culture are eliminated and European codes established instead (p.185).

Pagano (1990) makes a similar point. She comments on the strategies used by females to achieve academic success, asserting that girls and women are forced into silence in the educational context. Females, she argues, compromise their collective voice in exchange for academic success. Furthermore, their active participation in this process serves to reinforce the male image of female compliance.

Fordham (1993) draws similar conclusions in an ethnographic study of Black girls at Capital High, a predominantly Black high school in America. She describes the practice of silence as 'passing'. A major characteristic of passing is the denial of self, acting in ways which do not occur naturally in order to achieve academic success. She asserts that for Black girls this means imitating the norms of White American males and females. Fordham contends that gender passing has rarely been recognised as a factor in underperformance, despite the fact that educational research consistently shows that Black girls' achievements are greater than those of boys. High achieving girls, she reports, assume a 'ghostlike' existence characterised by silence and invisibility. They tend not to identify with the Black community and their test results are usually high. Low achieving girls, on the other hand, are highly visible and are often known throughout the school. Furthermore, they make no attempt to minimise their presence. They display strong cultural links with the Black community and their test results are generally low. Fordham, like Evans, concludes that Black female success is achieved at great cost, claiming that 'Black females pay an inordinate price for academic success; it leads to an 'ignorance of connections,' an uncertain 'fork in the road' (p. 24).

Other writers have pointed to the relationship between institutional racism in schools, sexism within minority communities and the effects this has on ethnic minority female students. Rezai-Rashti (1994:76), for instance, writing on the position of Asian pupils in the Canadian educational system observes:

> These students not only have to deal with the institutional racism present in the school system and in society at large but sometimes with sexist practices prevalent within their own communities and the racialisation of the gender issues at the school level.

She goes on to highlight the difficulties of approaches which fail to take into consideration the racist and sexist practices in the students' own communities and in the school, arguing that 'both worlds exhibit racism and sexism' (p.78). Although dealing specifically with the experience of Asian girls, her conclusions may well apply to Black girls too.

Research on Black boys

A popular 'image' of Black boys portrayed in the educational literature is of Patois speaking, underachieving and disaffected individuals (Edwards, 1986). Several studies have reported that teacher evaluations of Black boys are negative. Writing about teacher-pupil interactions in primary school, Wright (1986) observes that Black boys are often perceived as trouble-makers and a challenge to teacher authority. Black pupils, she argues, tend to act in stereotyped ways because of the negative labels given to them. She asserts that 'for Black pupils the school seemed to be seen as a 'battle ground', a hostile environment insofar as it rejects their colour and identity' (p. 133). A Black teacher in her study succinctly captures the popular image held of Black boys:

> The West Indian pupils, especially the boys are seen as a problem in this school because they are so 'aggressive'... I am using a quote here, they are so openly aggressive and surly (p. 132).

In a later study, Wright (1992) notes that teacher perceptions of Black boys as belligerent, arrogant and underachieving are deeply entrenched from the earliest years of schooling. A White teacher's daily log included the following, about a six year old boy of African-Caribbean origin:

> I think Robert [Justin's fellow pupil] may be in little pieces by the morning. He had an argument with Justin today and I've seldom seen a face like it on a little child. The temper, rage and marked aggression was quite frightening to see. I wouldn't be surprised in years to come if Justin wasn't capable of actually killing someone. When he smiles he could charm the birds off the trees, but when he's in a temper he is incapable of controlling himself. He has an extremely short fuse, is a real chauvinist and to cap it all he's got a persecution complex. He has to be handled with kid gloves.

This is about a six year old child! The teacher's interpretation of the incident highlights a generally held view of Black boys which may well adversely affect their educational outcomes.

Evidence that teachers hold stereotyped images of Black boys is also found by Gillborn (1988: 375) in his study of City Road comprehensive school. He notes that teachers hold opinions of Black boys' presumed aggressive nature which, in turn, influence their interactions. A head of year, for example, had the following to say about a pupil:

> He [Wayne Johnson] likes to steal the show, you know, he's *very arrogant*, will take advantage of the slightest possibility (...) He likes to drag people in with him. He likes to be the *showman*, the big guy, 'Look at me', you know. I can do this. I can do that' (original italics).

All the comments quoted above demonstrate deeply rooted prejudice and low teacher expectations. It is reasonable to assume that Black boys are highly sensitive to negative teacher evaluations and may unwittingly respond by acting out the stereotype.

Underperformance and gender

There is growing body of research which suggests that Black girls are performing better than Black boys (cf. Eggleston *et al*, 1986; Kysel, 1988). In her study based on Black girls nearing school leaving age in two London schools, Mirza (1992) challenges the stereotyped view of underachieving Black girls. She found that Black girls achieve a significant degree of success in the educational system. They do not, however, gain the economic status and occupational prestige commensurate with their qualifications and experience. Similarly, Black boys, while aspiring to high social class occupations, were less likely to have their ambitions realised in the job market.

The underlying reasons for Black pupils' differential educational outcomes in Britain have unfortunately attracted little scholarly attention. As we have seen, Black girls are more amenable to 'fitting in' with the dominant school ideology (Fordham, 1988). Consequently, they tend to achieve greater academic gains than Black boys. This is not to suggest that all boys fail, but Fordham's (1988) study showed that those boys who do succeed do so at enormous social, cultural and psychological cost. By disassociating themselves from things 'Black' and adopting a 'raceless' persona, Black boys were able to attain academic qualifications that were comparable to those of not only Black girls but also their White peers.

Some scholars, in an attempt to offer solutions for Black underachievement have resorted to distinctly pathological explanations. Mirza (1992) highlights the pitfalls of studies into the achievements of Black girls which, she argues, provide a 'distinctly pathological explanation' on the one hand, and a 'commonsense' explanation on the other. Some studies (eg Moynihan, 1965 reported in Rainwater and Yancey, 1967; Gibson and Barrow, 1986) point to the reputed matriarchal nature of the Black family which, they claim, cause it to be weak and dysfunctional. Others such as Fuller's (1982) point to the relationship between achievement and the centrality of the mother in the Black family. Studies of this kind emphasise the Black mother as the central force in shaping their daughters' aspirations. Both approaches, Mirza asserts, are based on similar grounds:

> Both theoretical positions, though they appeared outwardly to be constructed in opposition to each other, in effect draw on two similar assumptions: the presumed matriarchal structure of the Black family and the marginalisation of the Black male within that structure (p. 16).

The tendency to focus on the matriarchal nature of the Black family has also been observed by Black scholars who have attempted to offer solutions from a Black perspective. Jackson (1973) asserts that:

> Oft-cited myths about Black women and education purport that they are better educated than Black men, having received their education at the expense of Black men and being less threatening to the dominant power structure.

Jackson contends that matriarchal and emasculatory explanations of this kind serve as a mask for internalised White racism. Davis (1988) presents another view. Whilst working in Fulton, a working class district of Virginia, Davis observed that Black girls often attended high school away from home and were geared towards academic achievement, whereas boys were often found doing low skilled manual work. Additionally, he points to the practical difficulties an educated Black man living in an American community two generations away from slavery would face:

> It was widely remarked of William Armistead, for instance, 'If he had had an education, he would have been a genius.' It must have been only too clear that even a genius, if he were Black, would be forced to till the soil to earn a living (p. 25).

Studies such as these indicate that the explanation does not, in fact, lie with the family but is a product of the wider society. Thus, whilst Black pupils are underachieving overall, Black girls are in reality attaining levels which are comparable to other groups and achieve considerably more qualifications than Black boys. Furthermore, the mother in the Black family is perceived, rightly or wrongly, to have special characteristics which affect Black children's academic performance. Given the multifaceted role of gender in the education of Black children, it is important to ask how or whether Black teachers' cultural expectations of gender roles influence the relationships they have with Black children. Moreover, it is important to assess the ways in which this may be realised in the classroom context.

Gender, race and praise

In the previous chapter, the analysis of praise focused exclusively on ethnicity. Now we examine the interaction of gender and ethnicity.

Statistical analysis demonstrated that there were no significant differences in the amount of praise received by Black boys and White boys ($p = 0.085$). Further analysis of the interaction of gender and ethnicity support these findings ($p = 0.2118$).

Gender, race and blame

In chapter six we examined the effects of ethnicity on praise and blame and it emerged that Black children as a group were reprimanded significantly more than White children. This pattern was repeated when separate analyses were carried out for boys and girls.

Further analysis of the interaction of gender and ethnicity reveals that, of all the groups – Black boys, White boys, Black girls and White girls – Black boys receive most reprimands. This pattern was repeated when mild and severe blame were treated separately (mild blame: $p = 0.0072$; severe blame; $p = 0.0$). These findings confirm the subtle differences in teacher behaviour. Moreover, they confirm the findings of previous research which highlights the disproportionate amount of sanctions directed at Black boys (Gillborn, 1988, 1990a, 1990b; Wright 1986, 1987, 1992).

Teacher comments on gender and ethnicity

The findings of the quantitative analysis are mirrored in informal teacher comments. Pearlette Campbell suggested that Black girls try to compete with their White peers whereas Black boys are disinterested. And Leroy Wiltshire comments:

> I find that with Black girls there is a more positive response to work. They are very enthusiastic about their work, whereas the Black boys have a lackadaisical attitude. The boys are not as concerned about education as the girls.

The tendency for Black boys to be disinterested and less concerned with academic achievement was also observed by Winston Thompson:

> There is a distinct difference between the girls and boys. The girls will listen and try to improve – not the boys. The boys are more concerned with what he thinks of him as a footballer etc. When I look at them I know they have academic potential but they don't care about it. The Black girls are moving on much better than the Black boys.

Similarly, Evadne Sargeant reported that she treated Black boys differently, and was consciously aware of the reasons for her behaviour.

> When they come to my classroom I am hard with them. I speak to the parents and ask for their help. You have to be harder with the Black boys than we are with the girls. Black teachers know what is outside. Without an education Black boys have a problem. I make sure that I do not let them throw away what is rightfully theirs.

Deborah Lashley was unusual in claiming that she did not observe any differences between Black girls and boys. She asserts:

> There isn't really that much difference. You have some occasions where the Black boys work harder than the girls. Then you have another time when the girls are doing better than the boys.

The overall impression of the teachers, then, was that Black girls were more likely to respond positively in the classroom context than Black boys. Furthermore, statistical analysis shows that although Black girls received more reprimands than White girls they were reprimanded less than Black boys.

The observations made in my study arguably correspond in some respects to the research reviewed above. If we choose to infer that there is a relationship between the amount of reprimands received by Black girls compared with boys, it is plausible to assume that it is because they are better behaved. In fact, the qualitative data suggests that Black girls are more flexible regarding the demands of their teachers. But there is no evidence that Black boys and girls perceived any differences in the ways that they were treated by their teachers.

Two complementary questions arise. Firstly, to what extent can the position of Black girls and boys be attributed to a function of gender, in which females are often regarded as co-operative and males competitive? Secondly, are Black girls and boys socialised in different ways, ways which lead to their differential responses to the educational context?

Conclusion

Studies of the language socialisation of boys and girls indicate that the discourse directed towards young children varies according to the sender and recipient of the message. A result of this gender influenced behaviour is that the language patterns of boys and girls are firmly established prior to their entry to formal education. In an educational setting many writers have observed that boys dominate classroom discourse and use a range of strategies to ensure teacher attention. Further, teacher behaviour towards boys may tacitly reinforce this pattern.

In the case of Black children gender intersects ethnicity. Black children's presence in the educational literature is frequently linked to underperformance. Moreover, they are often portrayed as being loud, aggressive, surly and difficult to manage. Despite these negative evaluations, however, Black girls appear to make significantly more gains than Black boys.

Several explanations have been put forward to explain this phenomenon. Advocates of matriarchal and emasculatory theories highlight the centrality of the mother in the Black family and downgrade the role of Black fathers. These approaches have been criticised on grounds that they emanate from similar theoretical perspectives, which effectively marginalise the position of Black men.

The quantitative analysis of praising and blaming strategies across four dyads – Black boys and Black girls, White boys and White girls, Black boys and Black girls and White boys and White girls – presented in these pages indicates that there are no significant differences in the amount of praise received across the four groups. A multi-level analysis of blame, however, demonstrates a statistically significant relationship in the amount of severe blame directed at Black boys.

Teachers who took part in the study suggested a number of reasons why they treated Black boys differently from the girls. Some said that Black girls were more motivated and that Black boys tended to be lazy and disinterested. Others described their behaviour in terms of helping Black children to succeed. A recurrent feature, however, was the teacher's concern that Black children take advantage of the educational opportunities available to them.

Chapter 8
Conclusion

The impetus for this research was not only the extensive literature on underperformance and cross-cultural misunderstanding but also my own experience, first as a pupil and later as a teacher in British schools. I wanted to explore the teaching style of Black teachers in order to discover whether their practice differed from that of their White colleagues. Three questions guided my research from the outset: are Black teachers' interactions with Black children influenced by shared cultural knowledge? To what extent did Black teachers' and pupils' experience of school match my own? And what is the effect of Black teacher-pupil interactions on the learning experiences of Black children?

Underperformance

One of the main motives for undertaking research on Black teaching style was my concern about the continuing underperformance of Black children. This underperformance dates back to the early 1960s and continues today. In 1971, the publication of Coard's influential text *How the West Indian child is made educationally sub-normal in the British school system*, sharpened perceptions of the racist practices inherent in the British system which effectively labelled many Black children as mentally deficient and assigned them to the lower rungs of the educational ladder.

Official recognition of Black underperformance was slow, and in 1979 a government Committee of Inquiry was established to consider the causes of underachievement. The Rampton Report (DES, 1981) pointed to the low number of African-Caribbean children achieving examination passes and the tendency for Black pupils not to go on to courses of higher education. The findings of the second stage of this inquiry were published as the Swann Report (DES, 1985) and highlighted a marked improvement in Black achievement. But the overall pattern of Black underperformance remained unchanged.

Several explanations have been put forward in an effort to explain the underachievement of Black pupils. Advocates of early differentiation argue that Black children fall behind at an early stage in their educational careers and point to the organisation and practices of the primary school as possible contributory factors in underperformance. The treatment of Black pupils as a homogeneous group has also been identified as a factor. It has been argued, for instance, that researchers have failed to differentiate between various groups of children and in so doing have failed to consider important within-group differences.

Explanations of underperformance can be divided into three groups: functionalist, critical and interpretative. These explanations are closely linked to changing political ideologies. The functionalist perspective asserts that underperformance can be explained in terms of the effects of the individual pupils or their families on the schooling process. Ethnic minority groups are seen as 'deprived', 'deficient' or 'disadvantaged' and needing to be assimilated into the dominant culture.

Writers in the critical tradition, on the other hand, focus on the role of the school, asserting that education maintains a structure based on social inequality and that differences between minority and majority children therefore increase over time and reinforce the level of disadvantage of ethnic minority pupils.

Black researchers and those concerned with Black perspectives on underperformance argue that the groups concerned should be encouraged to find their own solutions to the problem. Interpretative studies of this kind offer a more holistic view. The relationship between Black underperformance, culture and caste, learning styles, effective Black teachers and achievement studies are among the topics which have been discussed by writers in this tradition. They have also highlighted the significance of 'community nomination', a methodological tool whereby members of minority communities nominate teachers whom they regard as being 'effective' in their teaching of Black pupils. Such research offers interesting insights into possible strategies for improving the educational performance of Black children.

The language debate

Language has also been identified, both as a possible factor in under-achievement and as a symbol of resistance to the dominant culture. The language spoken by children of Caribbean heritage in Britain was formed as a result of multilingual contact between African slaves and European slave-owners in the former West Indies. Traditionally, linguists argued that the pidgins and creoles which developed were an inferior version of standard English. During this century, however, this view has been refuted and the emphasis has changed from the alleged deficiencies of creoles to their significance in the debate on the ways in which human languages evolve (see, for example, Romaine, 1988).

The settlement of Caribbean peoples in the UK has added a further dimension to a situation which was already linguistically complex. Many terms have been used to describe the variety spoken by Black British children of Caribbean origin, including Black British English, Patois and British Jamaican Creole. The mushrooming of 'labels' in the last ten years or so is an indication of the complexity of the linguistic choices facing young Black Britons.

Links between language and identity have also received attention. The use of creole is seen as a powerful assertion of cultural identity. The question of whether young Black Britons use one variety or more has been central to the discussion. Writers agree that two codes exist: one Black and the other White. The definition of the Black variety, however, is contentious. Sebba (1993), for instance, categorically states that the Black variety is focused on Jamaican Creole. In the absence of a national survey claims of this kind need to be viewed with caution: they take no account of regional differences or the possibility that Black children may speak more than one Black variety.

Attitudes towards Black varieties have historically been very negative and have, unfortunately, been used in making judgements about the speakers of these languages. Early responses to language diversity in the classroom came in the form of two opposing hypotheses, deficit and difference. Exponents of the deficit hypothesis argued that children who spoke non-standard varieties of English were linguistically deficient and sought to compensate for their alleged difficulties. Advocates of the difference hypothesis refuted these claims and asserted that non-standard varieties were different from the standard but in no way deficient.

Other writers suggest that the difference and deficit theories have no relevance for Black children. Smitherman (1977) is one of those who highlights the fact that proficiency in standard English does not necessarily represent a guarantee for economic success, and argues that significant changes in educational policy will be necessary to counter-act the effects of institutional racism.

Many people feel that recent changes to educational policy in Britain and the National Curriculum will further disadvantage and marginalise ethnic minority children. The emphasis in the English documents on a monocultural society sharing a common heritage effectively marginalises the language and culture of many ethnic groups. One practical response to this situation has been suggested by proponents of 'critical language awareness' (eg Clark et al, 1990; 1991) who argue that children can be taught about language diversity in a way which raises issues such as social justice and equity.

Cultural style

More recent approaches to underperformance have highlighted the daily experiences of Black pupils in multi-ethnic schools. These studies have pointed firstly, to the ways in which differences in cultural style lead to miscommunication and, secondly, to the differential treatment received by Black children and White.

Writers concerned with cultural differences have pointed to the ways in which style is displayed through verbal and non-verbal communication patterns. They argue that Black discourse is interpersonal, animated and contrapuntal whereas White discourse is more impersonal and dis-passionate, and adheres to strict turn-taking conventions. Cultural style is also displayed through music and dress. Style, then, permeates all aspects of life.

Differences between Black and White cultural styles have important implications in the educational context. Studies in Britain and America have illustrated the ways in which displays of cultural style lead to miscommunication between Black children and White teachers. As a consequence, many Black British children, especially boys, are being referred to off-site units or being suspended or excluded from school. There is growing concern about this issue and several local education authorities have carried out their own investigations into the problem (CRE, 1985; Nottingham Advisory and Inspection Service, 1992).

Writers such as Wright (1992), Gillborn (1990a) and Biggs and Edwards (1991) claim that differences in discourse style can lead teachers to respond unfavourably to linguistic and cultural patterns which do not match their own. Much of this behaviour is quite subtle and although many teachers may claim that all of the children in their care receive the same treatment, the reality is that they do not.

Despite the evidence of widespread underperformance among Black children, many do succeed. Writers such as Fordham (1988) and Fordham and Ogbu (1986) suggest that academically successful Black pupils adopt a 'raceless' persona. Mac an Ghaill (1988) points to coping and survival strategies; and Fordham (1993) observes a tendency for Black girls to adopt a 'ghostlike' existence. There are also indications that Black children may pay a significant personal, social and psychological price in their search for academic success.

The framework for the present research

This book is based on data gathered from six Black teachers in two primary schools. Given that I was dealing with an area which has received little scholarly attention to date, I decided in the first instance to use an ethnographic framework which would generate hypotheses as part of the research process, rather than formulating hypotheses at the outset. However, after further reading and reflection, critical ethnography seemed a more suitable approach. Critical ethnography encourages researchers to make clear their ideological position and rejects the notion of a 'value free' stance. The central issue in my research, then, was whose interests were being served. Thus the challenge was twofold: could I ensure reliability in the data collection by minimising personal bias? And would I be able to make a contribution to the ongoing debate on Black children's underperformance by highlighting the situation of Black educators?

Catalytic validity, an essential characteristic of critical ethnography, holds that the research process should lead to increased awareness and the active participation of respondents. Accordingly, I sought to involve teachers and pupils by regularly feeding back information as part of the verification process. This activity also proved to be an invaluable checking device and provided clarification in areas of ambiguity.

The process enabled me to reflect on my practice as a teacher and has sharpened my perceptions of the ways in which I interact with pupils in the classroom. I have also been invited to the schools involved in order to disseminate the main findings of my study as part of an in-service programme of training for teachers.

Several methods of data collection were used. The period of fieldwork allowed me to establish my position as a researcher and created opportunities for me to make detailed fieldnotes. My ethnicity and my position as a Black researcher gave me valuable perspectives on the topic under investigation, and may have played a valuable part in gaining data which would have eluded a White researcher.

In the initial stages of fieldwork I acted as a 'natural observer'. Unlike participant observation, natural observation helps to guard against the risk of becoming too personally involved in the research process. There was, nonetheless, a degree of flexibility in my role, which meant that I was sometimes perceived as another adult to be called upon in a case of emergency, or an intimate with whom confidential matters could be shared. I was conscious at all times, however, of the effects of 'the observer's paradox'. In the later stages of fieldwork, observational data were supplemented with video-recordings of some sixty hours of classroom interaction.

Interviews with teachers and pupils created opportunities to focus on specific areas of interest and allowed the respondents to give their own interpretation of classroom events. This research method was particularly successful in eliciting teacher opinions and pupil perceptions on a range of topics.

Finally, quantitative research methods enabled me to investigate subtle aspects of teacher behaviour which had eluded qualitative analysis. The use of chi square, a statistical test for nominal data, allowed me to establish whether Black teachers behaved in statistically significantly different ways towards Black children and White and towards girls and boys.

Black communications

Much of the discussion of Black language in education has taken place in the context of African-American students and teachers in the USA. I was interested in establishing the extent to which 'Black communications' also played a part in British classrooms. Black communication goes well beyond matters concerning lexis, grammar and phonology to a range of non-verbal and paralinguistic features. All these features combine to make effective communication in the Black idiom.

For instance, call-response, the principle organising characteristic of African communication, is found in both sacred and secular contexts. In an educational setting it joins teachers and pupils into a community of learners. It establishes a high degree of rapport between teachers and pupils. It also encourages group participation and the establishment of shared norms. Call-response emerged as a clear characteristic of the teaching style of many of the Black teachers in the study.

Other characteristically Black speech events observed in teacher discourse included signifying, a form of humourous put-down which relies on a degree of circumlocution. Repetition was used to stimulate participation and restate information. Proverbs and moral teachings were also used as a teaching device in interactions with the children.

Non-verbal communication and paralinguistic features were equally important. Many teachers used their bodies, eyes and paralinguistic modes in addition to the spoken word. These strategies were particularly effective when used as part of Black teacher's control strategies. Both teachers and pupils were conscious of these African retained patterns in Black teachers' discourse. Teachers, for instance, reported that they tended to use Patois when reprimanding Black children. African retained features were thus a very important characteristic of Black teaching style with which Black children could culturally 'connect'.

Classroom control

Another focus for fieldwork was the ways in which Black teachers typically exerted classroom control. Discipline in school is enacted through a system of rewards and reprimands, of praise and blame. The system of discipline which operates in school, a White middle class institution, is often very different from the systems which operate in other cultural groups.

Many writers have pointed to the ways in which discipline is seen in the Black family as a part of the preparation of children for a world which refuses to accept them as equal citizens. As a result, what may appear to White observers to be an unnecessary scolding of a child may in fact be the teaching of an adaptive strategy.

Praise and blame have as their affective function the establishment and promotion of community values. I observed two types of praise: public and private. Public praise demonstrated teacher approval as well as the setting of communal norms. Private praise merely communicated teacher approval on a one-to-one basis. Black teachers adopted both private and public praise whereas White teachers tended to prefer private praising strategies. When the data for praise were subjected to statistical analysis, no significant relationships with ethnicity were found in teachers' praising strategies for children.

Black teachers' blaming strategies occurred along a continuum ranging from directness to truth-telling and served a variety of purposes. Directness is characterised by the explicit use of instructions. Truth-telling, on the other hand, is intended to embarrass the individual. It aims to reduce misbehaviour through the use of public sanction. Analysis of qualitative data indicated that there were differences in the ways that Black teachers and White reprimanded children, with only Black teachers tending to draw public attention to misbehaviour.

Pupils were often aware of and could articulate the differences in Black teacher behaviour as compared with White. They identified firm discipline as a characteristic of Black teachers and many reported that they valued this aspect of teacher behaviour. Others likened Black teachers' reprimanding strategies to the forms of discipline used in the home. They were also aware of the fact that Black teachers provided positive role models. In fact, some children who had not yet been taught by Black teachers commented that they wished they were.

White pupils also recognise differences between Black teachers and White, reporting that Black teachers gave them 'harder' work. Among White pupils, the teacher's ethnicity did not feature in their preferences. They were more concerned with the teacher's ability to relate to them as individuals. White pupils did not express any antipathy to Black teachers but my own ethnicity may have influenced their responses.

Remember, though, that Black teachers differentiate and are less firm in their treatment of White children.

Although Black teachers' praising strategies were the same for all children, I thought it would be interesting to consider whether the ethnicity or gender of children affected teachers' blaming strategies. Quantitative analysis did in fact indicate that Black children receive more blame than White children. Various reasons can be put forward to explain this differential behaviour. For example, the knowledge on the part of Black teachers of the disadvantages faced by Black children may lead them to respond in ways which are intended to help Black children achieve their full potential and prepare them for life in a hostile society. Other possible explanations for these patterns may lie in the 'connectedness' which Black teachers display towards Black children and their parents. This is discussed later in this chapter.

The effect of gender

Relationships between gender, culture and education have important implications for ethnic minority pupils' experiences of school. Many studies have pointed to the ways in which language socialisation leads to a situation where boys and girls acquire quite separate and distinctive language patterns. Furthermore, these patterns of language are established early in the child's life and well before they start formal education.

Research into language and gender has pointed to the ways in which girls are frequently marginalised in mixed classrooms. This has led some commentators (eg Spender, 1982) to conclude that it is not possible to treat boys and girls equally. Other studies have illustrated the role of teachers in maintaining male dominated discourse patterns in the classroom (Swann, 1988).

In the case of Black children, gender intersects ethnicity. Black boys are regularly caricatured as Patois speaking, disaffected and underachieving (Edwards, 1986); Black girls as 'loud' and 'difficult to manage' (Mirza, 1992). However, it would appear that Black girls are more skilled in manipulating their position in the school. Evans (1988), for instance, reports that whilst Black girls actively flout school rules, they do not actually break them.

Writers concerned with differences in the achievements of Black girls and boys have argued that the Black mother figure exerts considerable influence on the attainments of Black girls. Others point to the tendency for Black families to educate their girls at the expense of boys. Some Black commentators have even suggested that Black mother-son relationships are based on the notion that they 'love their sons' and 'raise their daughters' (Kunjufu, 1989). What is clear is that Black girls are attaining higher levels than Black boys. The reasons for these differential outcomes, however, are less than clear.

The Black girls in my study received significantly more blame than White girls. When blaming behaviours were categorised into 'mild' and 'severe', however, it was Black boys who received the most severe reprimands most often. This confirms the observations of writers such as Gillborn (1992) and Wright (1992) who point to the disproportionate amount of negative sanctions directed at Black boys.

Implications of the research

Throughout this study various themes emerged which have implications for furthering understanding of the underperformance of Black children. These can conveniently be divided into three main areas. Firstly, Black teaching style, secondly, issues which have methodological or peda-gogical implications, and lastly, areas for further research: disconnected-ness, language and achievement and the position of Black boys.

Black teaching style

Research on underperformance in Britain has tended to concentrate on the pupils and not the teachers. In fact, the role of Black teachers has not really been considered at all. Many qualified and experienced teachers came to Britain in the late 1950s. Education for them repre-sented a route to increased social status. But they were unable to obtain posts commensurate with their experience and qualifications and were forced to take on a range of menial jobs. Many did, nonetheless, even-tually gain entry to teaching but found that they were appointed to jobs with little security or opportunities for career development. Recent changes in educational policy such as new criteria for Section 11 fund-ing, have highlighted both the precarious position of Black teachers and the fact that they are often seen as 'professional ethnics' with special skills in dealing with Black children. Moreover, local management of schools, which places matters of recruitment and retention in the hands of governing bodies, has increased the vulnerability of Black teachers.

The findings of the present study would suggest that it is possible to speak in terms of an identifiable teaching style amongst Black teachers. Black teaching style manifests itself in similar ways to male and female speech styles. For instance, whilst men and women use language differently, it is not the case that all women or all men are restricted to a particular style. Rather, certain clusters of features are associated more closely with male or female speech. Similarly, Black teaching style is characterised by a clustering of behaviours which draw on several aspects of Black culture.

One feature of Black teaching style is the use of a range of African retained communication patterns such as call-response, repetition and signifying. Non-verbal communication is another important feature of Black teaching style. The use of body language, oculesics and para-linguistic cues are common in Black discourse. They are frequently misunderstood by White teachers and have been identified as one of the reasons for the disproportionate number of Black pupils excluded or suspended from British schools.

Black teachers use a range of culturally familiar verbal strategies as part of their reward and reprimanding strategies such as directness, shaming and truth-telling, which are are intended to harden Black children and prepare them for life in a society which is very often hostile.

Another feature of Black teaching style is the level of involvement with Black pupils. In the Black community, adults play an important role in setting community values and norms. They also support the family in regularising misbehaviour, thus acting as an external checking device. Connectedness may be demonstrated overtly and covertly in Black teachers' interactions with Black children, occurring explicitly as part of classroom discourse, or implicitly as part of the teacher's 'hidden curriculum'. For example, in their interactions with Black children, Black teachers may comment on behaviours which normally fall outside the domain of the school. These various patterns have been collectively described as 'connectedness' (M. Foster, 1989, 1991).

Pedagogical implications

Black teaching style thus incorporates a range of attitudes, behaviours and linguistic patterns which draw on the historical, social and economic experiences of the Black community. Several reasons can be put forward to explain why Black teachers adopt a distinctive teaching style. It is emancipatory in intent, reflecting Black teachers' desire that Black children make the most of their educational opportunities. Several teachers in my study felt that the educational system in Britain would inevitably fail a large number of Black children. Accordingly they perceived it as their duty as members of the Black community and as teachers, to ensure that the children in their care did not fail. This was an important part of their 'hidden curriculum'.

Style is culturally influenced and consequently many Black children and their parents expect Black teachers to behave in ways that are culturally familiar. In the context of the school, this may mean replicating some of the regulatory patterns found in the home. Teachers who fail to behave in culturally familiar ways may well be viewed with suspicion by members of the community. Black teachers' role as significant adults, their ways of communicating, behaving, rewarding and reprimanding are inextricably linked to their conception of a pedagogy which prepares Black children for the realities of life outside school. Black teachers may also use Black teaching style because it worked for them when they were children. Whilst it may appear to White observers that Black teachers are unusually firm, these interactions may hold different significance for members of the Black community.

Black teaching style is based on a value system which is very different from that of White teachers. The behaviours of Black teachers may consequently be interpreted as in direct opposition to that of their White colleagues and to the prevailing philosophy of the school. Black teachers' use of shaming and truth-telling strategies, for instance, may be perceived by White teachers as unnecessarily harsh. Thus Black teaching style represents a source of possible cultural misunderstanding. Although the educative goals of Black teachers and White are the same, the strategies which they adopt appear diametrically opposed.

Black teaching style may be anathema to some White colleagues but it is important that they recognise that Black teachers' behaviours are underpinned by the desire for Black children to reach their full potential and achieve academic success. White teachers therefore need to gain a greater understanding of the cultural meanings attached to Black teaching strategies. Part of this understanding includes the acknowledgment of the concerns of Black teachers, Black pupils and their parents. A broader understanding of the socio-cultural matrix of Black teachers is crucial if White teachers are fully to understand the strategies adopted by their Black colleagues.

Black teaching style comprises various features which are present to a greater or lesser extent in Black teachers. It is more pronounced in teachers trained in the Caribbean than in those who have qualified in the British system. Black teachers are not a homogeneous group and it is important to acknowledge that some Black teachers educated and trained in the UK will find aspects of Black teaching style unpalatable.

Black teacher style also has varying significance for children. Many Black pupils find Black teaching style emancipatory and culturally 'connect' with it and for them, Black teachers' behaviour represents an important support for learning. The children I observed who culturally connected with Black teaching style were able to draw parallels with their perceptions and expectations of teachers in the Caribbean and Africa and many said that they felt fortunate to be taught by a Black teacher. However, it is also important to acknowledge that not all Black children share these feelings: I found a small number who clearly rejected the behaviours associated with Black teaching style, possibly because they were reminiscent of the control strategies they associated with their parents.

Black teaching style and White children

Certainly I am not arguing that Black teachers should adopt Black teaching style in their interactions with White pupils. Some White pupils might perceive Black reprimanding strategies as a personal attack. Even though many White children are familiar with aspects of Black culture such as use of creole as a sign of friendship and solidarity, and teeth-sucking (cf. Hewitt, 1986), they might not fully appreciate or be able to fully understand the intentions of other aspects of Black teaching style and there is a real possibility of miscommunication.

The White children I observed were aware of differences between Black and White teaching styles but they made no negative comments about Black teachers. And it was the Black pupils who received significantly more reprimands than their White peers.

Good working relationships within a school can depend on shared understandings of the reasons why teachers operate in different ways. It is essential that White teachers appreciate the reasons for distinctively Black approaches to classroom control; namely their desire to prepare Black children for a life in a hostile society and to achieve the best possible academic results. It is also important that they understand that the strategies which they employ carry very different meanings for Black children, allowing them to 'culturally connect'.

Methodological implications

Two main points regarding my methodology require some attention. The first concerns the need to supplement qualitative with quantitative data; the second the role of Black researchers.

Qualitative vs quantitative research

During the course of the fieldwork certain aspects of Black teaching style proved difficult to analyse. It was relatively easy to describe the broad parameters but it was impossible to determine on the basis of qualitative analysis whether, for instance, Black teachers behaved in exactly the same way towards Black children and White, or they treated girls the same way as boys. Any differences which might exist were very subtle. In order to pursue this line of inquiry, I needed to use quantitative techniques.

I suspected at the outset that Black girls were treated more firmly than Black boys. The quantitative analysis demonstrated that the opposite was true. I had also suspected that Black children were treated more firmly than their White peers and here the quantitative analysis confirmed my suspicions. I was dealing, then, with very subtle differences which could be demonstrated only using quantitative methods. The situation was thus very similar to that in Biggs and Edwards' (1991) study of multiracial classrooms. Here, too, it was difficult to predict the outcomes of the qualitative analysis.

The role of Black researchers

Another issue emerging from my work is the role of Black researchers. There is growing trend within the interpretative tradition to encourage ethnic minority communities to construct their own social histories, so allowing them to offer their perspectives of underperformance. It is hoped that the present book makes a useful contribution to a body of research which already includes the work of Bhattacharya (1990), Sethi (1990), Brar (1991) Rahkit (1991) Channer (1996) and Nehaul (1996). It is an issue which has attracted increasing concern in the last ten years or so. Alladina (1986) highlighted the dominance of White researchers in research on issues of Black language and Edwards (1994) makes a similar point when writing about who is best qualified to research minority issues. She explains her decision as a White researcher to turn her attention away from issues concerning Black language to other concerns, and to concentrate instead on empowering Black graduate researchers.

Although this stance has widespread support, the low numbers of Black academics and postgraduate researchers indicate that exclusionary practices are still prevalent. This has led Troyna and Edwards (1992: 31) to assert that the situation 'can only be corrected by the development of a policy which explicitly and self-consciously addresses that centrality of Black academics to the research process'.

Future research

Throughout the thesis, various themes emerge which have implications for future research. The most pertinent issues are disconnectedness, language and achievement and the position of Black boys.

Disconnectedness

Black teachers pointed to the importance of parental support and cooperation in the education of Black children. They also suggested that Black parents may unwittingly contribute to their children's failure if they are not involved with the schooling process. I believe this could be leading to 'disconnectedness'. Disconnectedness is characterised by several factors, including minimal home-school liaison, distant relationships between pupils and teachers and antagonistic attitudes towards school on the part of pupils and, in some cases, their parents. It is further marked by low involvement on the part of parents as governors or members of Parent Teacher Associations. Also symptomatic of disconnectedness is a tendency for schools and parents to contact each other only when a problem arises.

The traditional role of the Black teacher includes the socialisation of Black children, the establishment of strong home-school links and an emphasis on mutual support which serves the interests of the child. In the present climate, however, this role appears to be diminishing in importance. The cumulative effects of disconnectedness may well have far-reaching implications for teachers, pupils and their parents.

Language and achievement

The importance of understanding linguistic, non-verbal and cultural styles is crucial to the debate on Black underperformance. Pupils whose cultural norms do not match those of the school are at risk. If the teacher perceives differences as a 'problem', they may respond to their pupils' diversity with negative attitudes, low expectations and culturally inappropriate teaching and assessment. Children, in turn, may unwittingly respond by acting in stereotyped ways in reaction to the negative labels attributed to them. The cumulative effects of cultural miscommunication are demonstrated in a number of ways, including low self-concept, poor attainments and a perception of the school environment as hostile.

Relationships, however, may be improved. By adopting a critical language awareness framework it is possible to work with both teachers and pupils. Teachers can be encouraged to explore their assumptions about language and culture and to look at the ways in which they might reduce misunderstanding. Pupils, for their part, could look at topics such as 'How we communicate with one another', focusing particularly on situations where there are differences in age, gender, ethnicity and social status. Pupils could also be encouraged to consider their role in the communication process.

So whilst schools have the responsibility to teach pupils about the behavioural codes of society they have a responsibility also to recognise the cultural misunderstandings which are currently causing friction. This also has implications for the initial training of teachers and for teachers' professional development.

The position of Black boys

The large numbers of Black boys being excluded or suspended from school constitute a crisis. From the time of their entry into British classrooms in the early 1960s, Black boys have been labelled as ESN, disruptive, aggressive, surly and looking for trouble. Recent figures published by the Department for Education show that exclusions rose from 2,910 in 1990-1991 to 3,833 in 1991-1992. It is estimated that the figures for 1992-1993 were as high as 8,000. Black boys represent just two per cent of the school population but they are four times more likely to be expelled and account for eight per cent of exclusions.

In inner cities such as London, the situation is even more alarming. A survey conducted as part of a BBC2 documentary on expulsions reported by Younge (1994) illustrates that as many as eleven London boroughs fail to monitor the ethnic background of excluded pupils. Furthermore, in one south London borough, he found that African-Caribbean boys comprise eight per cent of the school population but seventy per cent of those excluded.

The disproportionate number of Black male exclusions has led to a number of responses. Some subscribe to the view that Black boys' over-representation is a direct result of their misbehaviour. Others point to the effects of racist practices in schools and in teacher-pupil relationships.

The Black community and Black educators can play an important part in identifying the possible sources of the problem and work towards helping Black boys develop strategies that will aid their educational careers. The Black community urgently needs to address the real possibility that we may be raising our daughters to cope better with education than our sons. Are our girls and boys really equipped to face the many challenges which schooling brings? The teachers I worked with generally considered that Black boys were more disinterested in classwork than Black girls. The evidence would suggest that Black girls are more amenable to 'fitting in'. This is a recurrent observation in many British and American studies. The question of how much Black girls' success is a function of their gender, and how much is related to gender and ethnicity, clearly needs to be resolved.

Teachers can also help Black boys to develop strategies that lead to increased academic performance and the reduction in exclusions (see

Sewell, 1997). There is an urgent need for all teachers to examine why Black boys, in particular, develop attitudes that impact negatively on their education. Above all, they need to consider their own practice and examine whether they unwittingly contribute to the development of antagonistic attitudes in their interactions with Black boys.

At the beginning of this book I pointed out how few Black educators there are in British schools. Now, in conclusion, I return to this theme and related issues. My study has shown how six Black teachers in two multi-ethnic schools teach. These individuals were not specially chosen for the study nor are they 'unique' in their practice. They do nonetheless have a great deal to offer all the children they teach.

My own observations and experience suggest that it is not uncommon for many children to go through compulsory schooling and not be taught by any teachers from ethnic minority groups. In important ways, these teachers increase children's self-esteem and allow pupils from ethnic minority and majority backgrounds to develop a greater appreciation of diversity and cultural difference. Black and other ethnic minority teachers are invaluable in helping children to shape their own ideas about which individuals can hold roles of authority and influence. Without enough exposure to Black teachers, pupils are likely to characterise the teaching profession and the pursuit of academic goals as better suited to indigenous groups.

Many of the children I interviewed responded very positively to teachers who shared similar cultural backgrounds. These teachers increase motivation, promote personal and academic achievement and instil a strong and positive attitude towards learning. They set these goals for all children, but also realise that for Black children they may have to take extra action.

This study has raised important questions about teacher-pupil relationships and people who read this book may be disturbed by some aspects of Black teaching style. I do not propose to condone or criticise Black teaching style here. But sharing the experiences of the teaching staff at Stockland School is a way of highlighting for readers how their assessments of their practice reflect their success in teaching and learning and at the same time affect their sense of personal efficacy.

One year after completing the fieldwork, Stockland School was inspected by Her Majesty's Inspectorate (HMI). The school successfully passed its inspection and was highly praised for its value for money, high levels of academic achievement and good teacher-pupil relationships. There was however, one sentence hidden away in the body of the report to which I was particularly drawn. Although the OFSTED inspectors praised staff for their whole school approach to discipline and effective classroom management, they nonetheless commented upon their 'concern that the firm discipline imposed may be inhibiting for some children's development of self-discipline and independence'. My observations do not support this view.

How might the numbers of ethnic minority teachers be increased?

Whilst endorsing all efforts to widen the participation of Black and ethnic minority students in courses of initial teacher education, it is also important to examine how this may be achieved. I vividly remember listening to a former Black male headteacher talk about his frustration of being the arbiter for issues concerning Black children. He represented the kind of individual that the profession and schools so need. What was forgotten, however, were his needs. He summed up his position by saying: '*I don't want to be a role model – I want to be me*'.

I am acutely aware of the complexity of his position. Black teachers are valuable, indeed essential, to British schools but should not be appointed on the sole basis of providing 'role models' for Black children. Although apparently well-intentioned, such approaches often mean that Black staff end up with 'professional ethnic' status (Blair, 1993).

So it is not a case of simply increasing the numbers of ethnic minority staff. Black and other ethnic minority educators need to be visible at all levels so that they become part of the fabric of the educational process. I prefer to think in terms of 'peer modelling', where adults from the community and pupils in school work closely with successful ethnic minority educators.

There is no doubt that several factors – political, social and educational – have affected the declining numbers of ethnic minority teachers in the last decade. During the 1980s, Access courses set up in collaboration with further education colleges and initial teacher education institutions guaranteed a steady supply of mature Black and ethnic minority teachers. However, cuts in funding, in some cases, concern about the quality of these courses (and by implication their students) have greatly reduced the numbers of candidates able to enter the teaching profession via this route.

We already have evidence which shows that the average profile for an ethnic minority undergraduate student is that she is mature, Black and aged 25-39. It is, I suggest, wishful thinking to expect that the numbers of younger Black applicants will increase. That is, unless there is some reason for them to do so. Instead I propose a strategic programme involving ethnic minority communities, schools and colleges in collaboration with teacher training institutions.

Large scale national initiatives such as that carried out by the Higher Education Funding Council for Education (HEFCE) in 1993-1994 have proved difficult to measure in terms of their success and longer term effectiveness. What theoretically set out as an excellent and much needed initiative, turned out, in practice to provide very short-term solutions (cf. Showunmi and Constantine-Simms, 1995).

More recently the Teacher Training Agency (TTA) and the Commission for Racial Equality (CRE) have announced a series of national seminars to be held later this year. The seminars, entitled 'Teaching in Multi-Ethnic Britain: A Career for All', aim to look at ways in which the teaching profession can become more reflective of the multi-ethnic community it serves. This is indeed an important and much needed opportunity to debate matters of recruitment, retention, and the experiences of ethnic minority students and staff. It is to be hoped that these seminars will have long term follow up.

There are several examples of schemes aimed at raising the numbers of ethnic minority teachers in the USA. The Pathways to Teaching Program at Armstrong State and Savannah State Universities, for instance, involve collaboration between the school district, the local community, schools and two state colleges. Recruitment and admissions procedures have been designed to target individuals who may already have some involvement with schools and who wish to obtain certified teacher status. They are particularly concerned to increase the · number of ethnic minority men in the teaching profession.

Table 3: A model for increasing the numbers of ethnic minority students in teacher training

Students	• drawn from local schools/ further education colleges
	• identified through community nomination
Schools/Colleges	• encourage individuals who show potential
	• offer work shadowing so that interested individuals gain first hand experience
	• liaise with teacher training organisations
Teacher training institution	• recruits students (eg. from sixth form colleges and further education colleges)
	• places students in local schools where they receive the support of exemplary practitioners
	• offers advice sessions to prospective students
	• offers appropriate support mechanisms – study support, networking support groups etc
	• assesses faculty and curriculum development
	• creates opportunities for practising teachers to deliver curriculum
Local education authority	• undertakes to provide placements throughout the course that allow trainees access to professional development centres
	• receives an increased number of ethnic minority teachers each year
	• guarantees appointment on successful completion of the course (this could also include an undertaking by the trainee that they would work for a minimum of two or three years in LEA)
	• offers a programme of continuing professional development provided by teacher training organisation

The programme appears to provide benefits for all concerned. The students receive, among much else, networking support groups, orientation sessions, creative scheduling, workshops to improve skills, family support and tutoring/mentoring. The school system gains fifty five newly certified teachers per year, and there is a follow-up programme for newly qualified staff and ongoing collaboration with the teacher training providers. Importantly, the training institutions offer a curriculum relevant for urban environments, a significant increase in minority recruitment and retention, regular staff exchanges and increased collaboration between the two colleges.

In the British context the adoption of a strategy based on similar principles may offer an alternative and more permanent solution to this issue. Table 3 sets out one possible solution.

The model is designed to provide increased opportunities for collaboration between all parties involved in recruiting teachers. A major feature of the model is that it requires a commitment at all levels. All parties are proactive and will be involved in promoting teaching as a career. It differs from current practice in that there is increased emphasis on collaboration and partnership and, within the structure, each party has a sense of ownership. The model aims to shift the focus away from the limitations of potential candidates and onto the limitations of the institutions.

The value of this model is that it can be adapted to meet the needs of any group currently under-represented in the teaching profession. If, for instance, the aim is to increase the number of younger applicants it may be that the schools work with the teacher training providers to develop programmes where students gain direct access to existing students and academic faculty. If, on the other hand, the aim is to increase the number of male applicants it might be more profitable to work closely with community groups and workers in youth provision.

I suggest that this model be initially piloted in institutions and local education authorities where there is already demonstrable success in recruiting and retaining ethnic minority students. This will increase the chances for success. Whatever method, model or strategy is eventually adopted the overriding aim must be to bring more Black and ethnic minority teachers into schools and increase the numbers of successful and effective educators equipped to face the challenges of effective education in multi-ethnic society.

References

Abrahams, R. (1976) *Talking Black*. Rowley, MA: Newbury House

Achebe, C. (1980) *Things Fall Apart*. New York: Astor-Honor

Alladina, S. (1986) Black people's languages in Britain: a historical and contemporary perspective. *Journal of Multilingual and Multicultural Development* 7 (5): 349-359

Alexander, P. (1973) Normality. *Philosophy*. 48: 137-151

Au, K. (1980) Participation structures in a reading lesson with Hawaiian children: analysis of a culturally appropriate instructional event. *Anthropology and Education Quarterly* 11 (2): 91-115

Au, K. and Jordan, C. (1981) Teaching reading to Hawaiian children: finding a culturally appropriate solution. In H. Trueba, G. Guthrie and K. Au. (eds), *Culture in the Bilingual Classroom: Studies in Classroom Ethnography*. Rowley MA: Newbury House

Ausubel, D. (1968) *Educational Psychology: A Cognitive View*. New York: Holt, Reinhart and Winston

Ausubel, D. P, Novak, J. and Hanesian, H. (1978) *Educational Psychology: A Cognitive View*. New York: Holt, Rinehart and Winston

Baker, C. (1993) *Introduction to Bilingualism and Bilingual Education*. Clevedon: Multilingual Matters

Baumrind, D. (1972) An exploratory study of socialization effects on Black children: some Black-White comparisons. *Child Development* 74: 261-267

Bhattacharya, R. (1990) The Position of Black Teachers Today and the Future (unpublished). Commisioned paper for Open University course ED356, 'Race', Education and Society

Biggs, A., and Edwards, V. (1991) I treat them all the same: teacher-pupil talk in multiethnic classrooms. *Language and Education* 5 (3): 161-176

Blair, M. (1993) Black teachers, Black students and Education Markets. Paper presented at International Sociology of Education Conference, University of Sheffield, January.

Blair, M. and Maylor, U. (1993) Issues and concerns for Black women teachers in training. In I. Siraj-Blatchford (ed), *'Race', Gender and the Education of Teachers*. Buckingham: Open University Press, pp. 55-73

Boateng, F. (1980) African traditional education: a tool for intergenerational education. In M. Asante and K. Asante (eds), *African culture: the rhythms of unity.* Westport, CT: Greenwood Press

Bones, J. (1986) Language and Rastafari. In D. Sutcliffe and A. Wong (eds), *The Language of the Black Experience.* Oxford: Basil Blackwell

Bourne, J., Bridge, L. and Searle, C. (1994) *Outcast England: How Schools Exclude Black Children.* London: Institute of Race Relations

Bourdieu, P. (1966) *L'cole conservatrice.* Revue Francaise de Sociologie 7, 225-226; 330-342; 346-347

Bowles, S. and Gintis, H. (1976) *Schooling and Capitalist America.* London: Routledge and Kegan Paul

Bowles, S. and Gintis, H. (1982) IQ in the US class structure. In A. Finch, and P. Scrimshaw (eds), *Standards, Schooling and Education.* Sevenoaks: Open University in association with Hodder and Stoughton

Boykin, W. (1978) Psychological/behavioural verve in academic/task performance: pretheoretical considerations. *Journal of Negro Education* 47: 343-354

Boykin, W. (1994) Harvesting talent and culture: African-American children and educational reform. In Rossi, R (ed) *Schools and Students at Risk.* New York: Teachers College Press

Brandt, G. (forthcoming) British Youth Caribbean Creole – the politics of resistance. In T. Acton and M. Dalphinis (eds), *Superliterates and the Struggle for Multilingualism.* London: Karia Press

Brar, H. (1991) Unequal Opportunities: The Recruitment, Selection and Promotion Prospects for Black Teachers. *Evaluation and Research in Education* 5 (1 and 2): 35-47

Burstein, N. and Cabello, B. (1989) Preparing Teachers to Work with Culturally Diverse Students: Teacher Education Model. *Journal of Teacher Education* 40 (5): 9-16

Byers, P. and Byers, H. (1972) Non verbal communication and the education of children. In C. Cazden, V. John, and D. Hymes, (eds), *Functions of Language in the Classroom.* New York: Teachers College Press

Callender, C. and Cameron, D. (1990) Responsive listening as part of religious rhetoric: the case of Black pentecostal preaching. In G. McGregor and R. White (eds), *Reception and Response: Hearer Creativity in the Analysis of Spoken Discourse.* London: Routledge and Kegan Paul

Cameron, D. and Bourne, J. (1988) No Common Ground: Kingman, Grammar and the Nation. *Language and Education.* 2 (3): 147-160

Carby, H. (1980) *Multicultural Fictions.* Occasional Stencilled Paper No. 58, Centre for Contemporary Cultural Studies, University of Birmingham

Carranza, M. and Ryan, E. B. (1975) Evaluative Responses of Bilingual Anglo and Mexican American Adolescents Towards Speakers of English and Spanish. *International Journal of the Sociology of Language* 6: 83-104

Cazden, C. (1983) Can Ethnographic Research Go Beyond the Status Quo? *Anthropology and Education Quarterly* 14: 32-41

Cazden, C. (1988) Classroom Discourse: *The Language of Teaching and Learning.* Portsmouth, Heinemann

Channer, Y. (1996) *I am a Promise: the School Achievement of British African Caribbeans.* Stoke on Trent: Trentham Books

Clark, R., Fairclough, N., Ivanic, R. and Martin-Jones, M. (1990) Critical Language Awareness. Part 2: A Critical Review of Three Current Approaches to Language Awareness. *Language and Education.* 4: 249-260

Clark, R., Fairclough, N., Ivanic, R. and Martin-Jones, M. (1991) Critical Language Awareness. Part 2: Towards Critical Alternatives. *Language and Education* 5: 41-54

Cohen, R. (1969) Conceptual Styles, Culture Conflict, and Nonverbal Tests of Intelligence. *American Anthropologist* 71:828-856

Collins, M. and Tamarkin, C. (1982) *Marva Collins' Way.* New York: Tarcher Inc

Commission for Racial Equality. (1985) *Birmingham Local Education Authority and Schools: Referral and Suspension of Pupils.* London: CRE

Constantine-Simms, D. (1995) The Role of the Black Researcher in Educational Research. In V. Showunmi and D. Constantine-Simms (eds), *Teachers for the Future.* Stoke on Trent: Trentham Books

Cooke, B. (1980) Non verbal communication among Afro-Americans: an initial classification. In R. Jones, (ed), *Black Psychology.* New York: Harper and Row

Corson, D. (1993) *Language, Minority Education and Gender.* Clevedon: Multilingual Matters

Cronbach, L. and Snow, R. (1977) *Aptitudes and Instructional Methods.* New York: Irvington Publishers

Cruikshank, J. (1916) *Black Talk, Being Notes on Negro Dialect in British Guiana.* Georgetown: Argosy

Culver, S, Wolfle, L. and Cross, L. (1990) Testing a model of teacher satisfaction for Blacks and Whites. *American Educational Research Journal* 27 (2): 323-349

Dandy, E. (1991) *Black Communications: Breaking Down the Barriers.* African American Images: Chicago

Dalphinis, M. (1991) The Afro-English speech community. In S. Alladina and V. K. Edwards (eds), *Multilingualism in the British Isles: Africa, the Middle East and Asia.* Harlow: Longman

Daunt, P. (1975) *Comprehensive Values.* London: Heinemann

Davis, S. (1988) *The World of Patience Gromes: Making and Unmaking of a Black Community.* Lexington: University of Kentucky Press

Denscombe, M. (1985) *Classroom Control: A Sociological Perspective.* London: Allen and Unwin

Dent, D. (1989) Readin', Ritin' and Rage – How schools are destroying Black boys. *Essence* 20 (7): 54, 56, 59, 116

Department of Education and Science. (DES) (1985) *Education for All* (Swann Report). London: HMSO

Department of Education and Science. (DES) (1988) *Report of the Committee of Inquiry Into the Teaching of the English Language* (Kingman Report). London: HMSO

Department of Education and Science. (DES) (1989) *Discipline in Schools* (Elton Report). London: HMSO

Docking, J. (1987) *Control and Discipline in Schools: Perspectives and Approaches.* London: Harper and Row

Dodd, S. (1993) Down we go. *The Money Index.* January 12th

Domino, G. (1971) Interactive effects of achievement orientation and teaching style on academic achievement. *Journal of Educational Psychology* 62 (5): 427-431

Dumont, R. (1972) Learning English and how to be silent: studies in Sioux and Cherokee classrooms. In C. Cazden, V. John, and D. Hymes (eds), *Functions of Language in the Classroom.* New York: Teachers College Press (Reprinted by Waveland Press, 1985)

Durkheim, E. (1961) *Moral Education.* Glencoe, Ill: Free Press

Edwards, D. and Mercer, N. (1987) *Common Knowledge: The Development of Understanding in the Classroom.* London: Routledge

Edwards, J. (1979) *Language and Disadvantage.* London: Edward Arnold

Edwards, V. (1976) *West Indian Language, Attitudes and Underperformance in West Indian Children.* London: National Association for Multicultural Education

Edwards, V. (1979) *The West Indian Language Issue in British Schools.* London: Routledge and Kegan Paul

Edwards, V. (1986) *Language in a Black Community.* Clevedon: Multilingual Matters

Edwards, V. (1994) Edwards on Edwards: A Question of Relative Priorities. *International Journal of the Sociology of Language* 110: 187-192

Edwards, V. and Redfern, A. (1994) *The World in a Classroom: Language Education in Britain and Canada.* Clevedon: Multilingual Matters

Edwards, V. and Sienkewicz, T. (1990) *Oral Cultures Past and Present.* Oxford: Basil Blackwood

Eggleston, J., Dunn, D. and Anjali, M. (1986) *Education For Some: The Educational and Vocational Experiences of 15-18 year Old Members of Minority Ethnic Groups.* Stoke on Trent: Trentham Books

Erickson. F. (1987) Transformation and school success: the politics and culture of educational achievement. *Anthropology and Education Quarterly* 18 (4): 336-355

Evans, G. (1988) Those loud Black girls. In D. Spender and E. Sarah, (eds), *Learning To Lose: Sexism and Education.* London: The Women's Press

Fairclough, N. (1989) *Language and Power.* London: Longman

Foley, D. (1991) Reconsidering anthropological explanations of ethnic school failure. *Anthropology and Education Quarterly* 22 (1): 60-86

Foner, N. (1978) *Jamaica Farewell: Jamaican Migrants in London.* London: Routledge and Kegan Paul

Ford, D (1995) A study of underachievement among gifted Black students. Paper presented at the Annual Meeting of the American Educational Research Association, April, New York

Fordham, S. (1988) Racelessness as a factor in Black students' school success: pragmatic strategy or Pyrrhic victory. *Harvard Educational Review* 58 (1): 54-84

Fordham, S. (1993) 'Those loud Black girls': (Black) women, silence, and gender 'passing' in the academy. *Anthropology and Education Quarterly* 24 (1): 3-32

Fordham, S. and Ogbu, J. (1986) Black students' school success: coping with the burden of 'acting White'. *The Urban Review* 18 (3): 176-206

Foster, M. (1989) It's cookin' now: A performance analysis of the speech events of a Black teacher in an urban community college. *Language in Society* 18 (1): 1-29

Foster, M. (1990) The politics of race: through the eyes of African-American teachers. *Journal of Education* 172 (3): 123-141

Foster, M. (1991) Constancy, connectedness and constraints in the lives of African-American teachers'. *NWSA Journal* 3 (2): 233-261

Foster, P. (1990) Cases not proven: an evaluation of two studies of teacher racism. *British Educational Research Journal* 16 (4): 335-349

Foster, P. (1991) Cases still not proven: a reply to Cecile Wright. *British Educational Research Journal* 17 (2): 165-170

Foster, P. (1992a) Teacher attitudes and Afro-Caribbean educational attainment. *Oxford Review of Education.* 18 (3): 269-281

Foster, P. (1992b) Equal treatment and cultural difference in multiethnic schools: a critique of teacher ethnocentrism theory. *International Studies in Sociology of Education* 2 (1): 89-103

French, J. and French, P. (1993) Gender imbalances in the primary classroom: an interactional account. In P. Woods and M. Hammersley (eds), *Gender and Ethnicity in Schools: Ethnographic Accounts.* London: Routledge

Fuller, M. (1980) Black girls in a London comprehensive school. In R. Deem (ed), *Schooling for Women's Work.* London: Routledge and Kegan Paul

Fuller, M. (1982) Young, female and Black. In E. Cashmore and B. Troyna (eds), *Black Youth in Crisis.* London: Allen and Unwin

Garcia, O. and Otheguy, R. (1991) *English Across Cultures: Cultures Across English.* Berlin: Mouton de Gruyter

Gay, G (1975) Cultural differences important in the education of Black children. *Momentum.* (2): 322-340

Gibson, A. and Barrow, J. (1986) *The Unequal Struggle: The Findings of a West Indian Research Investigation Into the Underachievement of West Indian Children in British Schools.* London: Centre for Caribbean Studies

Gibson, M. and.Ogbu, J. (eds), (1991) *Minority Status and Schooling: A Comparative Study of Immigrant and Involuntary Minorities.* New York: Garland Publishing

Giles, H., Bourhis,R., Trudgill, P. and Lewis, A. (1974) The imposed norm hypothesis: a validation. *Quarterly Journal of Speech* 60: 405-410

Gillborn, D. (1988) Ethnicity and educational opportunity: case studies of West Indian male-White teacher relationships. *British Journal of Sociology of Education* 9 (4): 371-385

Gillborn, D. (1990a) When cultural display is seen as a challenge: ethnic minorities. *Times Educational Supplement*, 30th November: 10

Gillborn, D. (1990b) *Race, Ethnicity and Education: Teaching and Learning in Multi-Ethnic Schools*. London: Unwin Hyman

Gillborn, D. and Drew, D. (1992) Race, Class and School Effects. *New Community* 18 (4): 551-565

Gilroy, B. (1976) *Black Teacher*. London: Cassell

Goodson, I. (1992) *Studying Teachers' Lives*. London: Routledge and Kegan Paul

Graddol, D. and Swann, J. (1988) Trapping linguists: an analysis of linguists' responses to John Honey's pamphlet 'The language trap'. *Language and Education* 2: 95-111

Graduate Teacher Training Registry (1995) *Annual Statistical Report, Autumn 1995 Entry*. Cheltenham

Graduate Teacher Training Registry (1996) *Annual Statistical Report, Autumn 1996 Entry*. Cheltenham

Green, H. (1971) Socialization values in West African, Negro and East Indian cultures: a cross-cultural comparison. *Journal of Cross-cultural Psychology* 2: 309-312

Green, P. (1985) Multi-ethnic teaching and the pupils' self-concepts. In *Swann Report*. DES (1985), pp. 46-56

Guy, W. and Menter, I. (1992) Local management of resources: who benefits? In D. Gill, B. Mayor and M. Blair (eds), *Racism and Education: Structures and Strategies*. London: Sage

Hale-Benson, J. (1986) *Black Children: Their Roots, Culture and Learning Styles*. Baltimore: John Hopkins University Press

Hammersley, M. and Atkinson, P. (1991) *Ethnography: Principles in Practice*. London: Routledge

Hammersley, M. and Gomm, R. (1993) A response to Gillborn and Drew on 'race', class and school effects. *New Community* 19 (2): 348-353

Heath, S. (1983) *Ways With Words: Language, Life and Work in Communities and Classrooms*. Cambridge: Cambridge University Press

Hegarty, S. (1989) *Boosting Educational Achievement: report of the independent inquiry into educational achievement in the London borough of Newham*. London: Newham Council Education Committee

Henderson, D. and Washington, A. (1975) Cultural differences and the education of Black children: An alternative model for program development. *Journal of Negro Education* 44: 353-360

Hewitt, R. (1986) *White Talk Black Talk: Inter-Racial Friendship and Communication Amongst Adolescents*. Cambridge: Cambridge University Press

Hill, R. (1972) *The Strengths of Black Families*. New York: Emerson Hall

Hill-Collins, P. (1986) Learning from the outsider within: the sociological significance of Black feminist thought. *Social Problems* 33 (6): 14-32

Hilliard, A. (1985) Kemetic concepts in education. In I. Van Sertima (ed), Nile valley civilisations. Atlanta: *Journal of African Civilisation*, pp 153-162

Hilliard, A. (1989) Teachers and cultural styles in a pluralistic society. Issues 89: *NEA TODAY* 7 (6):65-69

Hollins, E. (1982) The Marva Collins story revisited: implications for regular classroom instruction. *Journal of Teacher Education* 33 (1):37-40

Holloway, J.(1991) *Africanisms in American Culture*. Indiana: Indiana University Press

hooks, b. (1993) *Sisters of the Yam: Black Women and Self-Recovery*. London: Turnaround

Hoover, M. (1985) Ethnology of Black Communications. *Journal of Black Reading/Language Education* 2: 2-4

Hubah, L. (1984) The position of Black teachers in this society. In *Challenging Racism*. London: (ed), ALTARF

Hudson, R. (1983) *Sociolinguistics*. Cambridge: Cambridge University Press

Husband, C. (1982) *'Race' in Britain: Continuity and Change*. London: Hutchinson

Hymas, C. and Thomas, L. (1994) Africans move to the top of Britains education ladder. *The Sunday Times* 23rd January:10.

Irvine, J. (1990) *Black Children School Failure: Policies, Practices and Prescriptions*. New York: Greewood Press

Irwin, R. (1977) Judgements of vocal quality, speech, fluency and confidence of southern Black and White speakers. *Language and Speech* 20: 261-266

Jackson, J.J. (1973) Black women in a racist society. In C. Willie, B. Kramer and B. Brown (eds), *Racism and Mental Health*. Pittsburgh: University of Pittsburgh Press

Jackson, L. (1986) Proverbs of Jamaica. In D. Sutcliffe and A. Wong (eds), *The Language of the Black Experience*. Oxford: Blackwell

John, G. (1993) Building on strengths, eliminating weaknesses: a developmental perspective. Paper presented to Asian and African-Caribbean teachers. London Borough of Hackney. October

Kagan, J. (1964) American longtitudinal research on psychological development. *Child Development* 35: 1-32

Katz, (1985) The sociopolitacal nature of counselling. *Counselling Psychologist* 13: 615-624

Kenway, P (1994) *Working with Parents*. University of Reading: Reading and Language Information Centre

Klein, G. (1951) The personal world through perception. In R. Blake and G. Ramsey (eds), Perception: *An Approach to Personality*. New York: Ronald Press, pp. 328-335

Kochman,T. (1981a) *Black and White styles in conflict*. Chicago: University of Chicago Press

Kochman, T. (1981b) 'Fighting Words' Black and White. Unpublished paper, University of Illinois, Chicago

Kunjufu, J. (1986a) *Countering the Conspiracy to Destroy Black Boys* (Vol 1). Chicago: African American Images

Kunjufu, J. (1986b) *Countering the Conspiracy to Destroy Black Boys* (Vol 2). Chicago: African American Images

Kunjufu, J. (1989) *Critical Issues in Educating African American Youth: A Talk with Jawanza*. Chicago: African American Images

Kysel, F. (1988) Ethnic background and examination results. *Educational Research* 30 (2): 83-89

Ladson-Billings, G. (1991) Returning to the source: implications for educating teachers of Black students. In M. Foster (ed), *Qualitative Investigations into School and Schooling*. New York: AMS Press

Ladson-Billings, G. (1990) Like lightning in a bottle: attempting to capture the pedagogical excellence of successful teachers of Black students. *Qualitative Studies in Education* 3 (4): 335-344

Ladson-Billings, G. and Henry, A. (1990) Blurring the borders: voices of African liberatory pedagogy in the United States and Canada. *Journal of Education* 172 (2): 72-88

Lambert, W. (1967) A social psychology of bilingualism. *Journal of Social Issues* 23 (2): 91-109

Lambert, W., Hodgson, R., and Fillenbaum, S. (1960) Evaluation reactions to spoken languages. *Journal of Abnormal and Social Psychology* 60: 44-51

Lein, L. (1975) Black American migrant children: their speech at home and school. *Anthropology and Education Quarterly* 6: 1-11

Lightfoot, S. (1973) Politics and reasoning: through the eyes of teachers and children. *Harvard Educational Review* 43 (2): 197-244

Lorde, A. (1982) *Zami*. Freedom CA: Crossing Press

Lowenthal, D. (1972) *West Indian Societies*. London: Oxford University Press

Lyons, N. (1983) On self, relationships and morality. *Harvard Educational Review* 53 (2): 125-145

Mabey, C. (1981) Black British literacy: a study of reading attainment of London Black children from 8 to 15 years. *Educational Research* 23 (2): 83-95

Mac an Ghaill, M. (1988) *Young, Gifted and Black: Student Teacher Relations in the Schooling of Black Youth*. Milton Keynes: Open University Press

Mac an Ghaill, M. (1992) Coming of age in 1980s England: reconceptualising Black students' schooling experience. In D. Gill, B. Mayor and M. Blair (eds), *Racism and Education: Structures and Strategies*. London: Sage

McDermott, R. (1987) The explanation of minority school failure again. *Anthropology and Education Quarterly* 18 (4): 336-367

Mahoney, P. (1985) *Schools for the Boys?* London: Hutchinson

Mascias, J. (1987) The hidden curriculum of Papago teachers: American Indian strategies for mitigating cultural discontinuity in early schooling. In G. Spindler and L. Spindler (eds), *Interpretive Ethnography at Home and Abroad*. Hillsdale, NJ: Lawrence Erlbaum Associates, pp. 363-380

Mbiti, J. (1990) *African Religions and Philosophy*. Portsmouth, NH: Heinnemann Educational

Mehan, H. (1993) Why I like to look: on the use of videotape as an instrument in educational research. In M. Schratz (ed), *Qualitative Voices in Educational Research*. Lewes: Falmer

Michaels, S. and Cazden, C. (1986) Teacher/child collaboration as oral preparation for literacy. In Schiefflin, B.and Gilmore, P. (eds), *The Acquisition of Literacy: Ethnographic Perspectives*. Norwood, NJ: Ablex

Michaels, S. and Collins, J. (1984) Oral discourse styles: classroom interaction and the acquisition of literacy. In D. Tannen (ed), *Coherance in Written and Spoken Discourse*. Norwood, NJ: Ablex

Miller, P. (1986) *Nonverbal Communication*. Washington DC: National Education Association

Mirza, H. (1992) *Young, Female and Black*. London: Routledge

Mitchell, H. (1970) *Black Preaching*. Philadelphia and New York: Lippincott and Kegan Paul

Mitchell, H. (1990) *Black Preaching: the Recovery of a Powerful Art*. Nashville: Abingdon Press

Mitchell-Kernan, C. (1972) Signifying and marking: two Afro-American speech acts. In T. Kochman (ed), *Rappin' and Stylin' Out: Communication in Urban Black America*. Urbana: University of Illinois Press

Mohatt, G. and Erickson, F. (1981) Cultural differences in teaching styles in an Odawa school: a sociolinguistic approach. In H. Trueba, G. Guthrie and K. Au (eds), *Culture in the Bilingual Classroom: Studies in Classroom Ethnography*. Rowley MA: Newbury House

Munroe, R. and Munroe, R. (1977) Cooperation and Competition among East-African and American children. *Journal of Social Psychology* 101:145-146

Nehaul K. (1996) *The Schooling of Children of Caribbean Heritage*. Stoke on Trent: Trentham Books

Nottingham County Council Education Department. (1992), *Pupil Exclusions from Nottingham Secondary Schools: Full Report*. Nottingham Education Department: Advisory and Inspection Service

Ogbu, J. (1974) *The Next Generation: An Ethnography of Education in an Urban Neighbourhood*. New York: Academic Press

Ogbu, J. (1978) *Minority Education and Caste: the American System in Cross-Cultural Perspective*. New York: Academic Press

Ogbu, J. (1981) School ethnography: a multilevel approach. *Anthropology and Education Quarterly* 12 (1): 3-29

Ogbu, J. (1987) Variability in minority school performance: a problem in search of an explanation. *Anthropology and Education Quarterly* 18 (4): 312-334

Ogilvy, C., Boath, E., Cheyne, W., Jahoda, C. and Schaffer, H. (1992) Staff-child interaction styles in multi-ethnic nursery schools. *British Journal of Developmental Psychology* 19: 85-97

Pagano, J. (1990) *Exiles and Communities: Teaching in the Patriarchal Wilderness.* Albany: State University of New York Press

Philips, S. (1983) *The Invisible Culture: Communication in Classroom and Community on the Warm Springs Indian Reservation.* New York: Longman

Philips, S., Steele, S. and Tanz, C. (eds), (1987) *Language, Gender and Sex in Comparative Perspective.* Cambridge: Cambridge University Press

Piestrup, A . (1974) Black dialect interference and accomodation of reading instruction in first grade. Language Behaviour Research Laboratory Monographs, vol. 4. Berkeley: University of California

Rainwater, L. and Yancey, W. (1967) *The Moynihan Report and the Politics of Controversy.* Cambridge, Mass: MIT Press

Ramirez, M. and Castaneda, A. (1974) *Cultural Democracy, Bicognitive Development and Education.* New York: Academic Press

Reisman, K. (1974) Contrapuntal conversations in an Antiguan village. In Bauman, R. and J. Sherzer (eds), *Explorations in the Ethnography of Speaking.* Cambridge: Cambridge University Press

Rezai-Rashti, G. (1994) The dilemma of working with minority female students in Canadian high schools. *Canadian Woman Studies/ les cahiers de la femme* 14 (2): 76-82

Rhakit, A. (1991) Black teachers' lives and careers. Unpublished MA dissertation, University of Warwick.

Rickford, J. and Rickford, A. (1976) Cut eye and suck teeth: African words and gestures in new world guise. *Journal of American Folklore* July -Sept: 294-309

Rist, R. (1970) Student social class and teacher expectations: the self-fulfilling prophecy in ghetto education. *Harvard Educational Review* 40 (3): 411- 451

Roberts, P. (1988) *West Indians and Their Language.* Cambridge: Cambridge University Press

Rosen, H. and Burgess, T. (1980) *Language and Dialects of London School Children: an investigation.* London: Ward Lock Educational

Rosenburg, B. (1988) *Can these Bones Live? The Art of the American Preacher.* Chicago: University of Illinois Press

Runnymede Trust (1994) *Multi-Ethnic Britain: Facts and Trends.* London

Sadker, M. and Sadker, D. (1985) Sexism in the schoolroom of the 80s. *Psychology Today* (March): 54-57

Scarr, S., B. Caparulo, B. Frerdman, B.Towers and Caplan, B. (1983), Developmental status and school achievements of minority and non-minority children from birth to 18 in a British Midlands town. *British Journal of Developmental Psychology* 1 (1): 31-48

Sebba, M. (1986) London Jamaican and Black London English. In *The Language of the Black Experience*. D. Sutcliffe and A. Wong (eds), Oxford: Basil Blackwell

Sebba, M. (1993) *London Jamaican*. Harlow, Essex: Longman

Sebba, M. and Tate, S. (1986) You know what I mean? Agreement marking in British Black English. *Journal of Pragmatics* 10: 163-172

Sethi, A. (1990) Black teachers. Unpublished paper, Holland Park and West London Teachers Group

Shade, B. (1982) Afro-American cognitive style: a variable in school success? *Review of Educational Research* 52 (2): 219 - 244

Silberman, C. (1973) *Crisis in the Classroom: the Remaking of American Education*. London: Wildwood House

Simon, R.I. and Dippo, D. (1986) On critical ethnographic work. *Anthropology and Education Quarterly* 17: 195-202

Smitherman, G (1977), *Talkin' and Testifyin': the Language of Black America*. Boston: Houghton Mifflin

Spender, D. (1982) *Invisible Women: the Schooling Scandal*. London: Writers and Readers Publishing Cooperative

Spindler, G. (1988) *Doing the Ethnography of Schooling*. Prospect Heights: Waveland Press

Spradley, B. (1979) *The Ethnographic Interview*. New York: Holt, Rinehart and Winston, Inc

Stack, B. (1974) *Strategies for Survival in a Black Community*. New York: Harper and Row

Steele, S. (1993) Water come a mi eye. *Language Matters* 3: 13-14

Stone, M (1981) *The Education of the Black Child: the Myth of Multiracial Education*. London: Fontana

Strickland, S. (1991) Black body language gets pupils into trouble. *The Independent*, 11th July: 2

Sutcliffe, D. (1982) *British Black English*. Oxford: Basil Blackwell

Sutcliffe, D. (1992) *System in Black Language*. Clevedon: Multilingual Matters

Sutcliffe, D. and Tomlin, C. (1986) The Black Churches. In D. Sutcliffe and A. Wong (eds) *The Language of the Black Experience*. Oxford: Basil Blackwell

Swann, J. (1988) Talk Control: an illustration from the classroom of problems in analysing male dominance of conversation. In J. Coates and D. Cameron (eds), *Women in their Speech Communities*. Harlow: Longman

Swann, J. and Graddol, D. (1988) Gender inequalities in classroom talk. *English in Education* 22 (1): 48-65

Taylor, O. (1990) *Cross-Cultural Communication: An Essential Dimension of Effective Education*. Washington DC: Mid-Atlantic Center for Race Equity

Thomas, J. (1993) *Doing Critical Ethnography*. Newbury Park, CA: Sage

Tizard, B., Blatchford, P., Burke, J., Farquhar, C. and Plewis, I. (1988) *Young Children at School in the Inner City*. London: Lawrence Erlbaum Associates

Tomlin, C. (1994) Black language style in sacred and secular contexts. Unpublished PhD thesis, Department of Arts and Humanities, University of Reading

Troyna, B. (1991) Underachievers or underrated? The experience of pupils of south Asian origin in a secondary school. *British Educational Research Journal* 17 (4): 361-376

Troyna, B. and Edwards, V. (1992), *The Educational Needs of a Multiracial Society*. Warwick: Centre for Research on Ethnic Relations

Tucker, G. R and Lambert, W. (1969) White and negro listeners' reactions to various American-English dialects. *Social Forces* 47: 463-468

Universities and Colleges Admissions Services (1995) *Statistical Bulletin*. Cheltenham

Walker, R. (1990) *Doing Research: A Handbook for Teachers*. London: Routledge

Watson-Gegeo, K. A. (1988) Ethnography in ESL: defining the essentials. *TESOL Quarterly* 22 (4): 575-593

Werner, O. and Schoepfle, G. M. (1987) *Systematic fieldwork: Vol 1: Foundation of ethnography and interviewing; Vol. 2 Ethnographic analysis and data management*. Newbury Park, CA: Sage

Whyte, J. (1986) *Girls into Science and Technology: the Story of a Project*. London: Routledge and Kegan Paul

Witkin, H. (1962) Origins of cognitive styles. In Scherer, C (ed), *Cognition: Theory, Research and Promise*. New York, Harper and Row, pp. 127-205

Witkin, H., Moore, C., Goodenough, D. and Cox, P. (1977) Field-dependent and field-independent cognitive styles and their educational implications. *Review of Educational Research* 47 (1): 1-64

Wong, A. (1986) Creole as a language of power and solidarity. In *The Language of the Black Experience*. D. Sutcliffe and A. Wong (eds), Oxford: Basil Blackwell

Woods, P. (1991) *Inside Schools: Ethnography in Educational Research*. London: Routledge and Kegan Paul

Wright, C. (1986) School processes: an ethnographic study. In J. Eggleston, D, Dunn and M. Anjali (eds), *Education for Some: the Educational and Vocational Experiences of 15-18 Year Old Members of Minority Ethnic Groups*. Stoke on Trent: Trentham Books

Wright, C. (1987) Black Students – White Teachers. In B. Troyna (ed), *Racial Inequality in Education*. London: Routledge and Kegan Paul

Wright, C. (1992) Early education: multiracial primary school classrooms. In D. Gill, B. Mayor and M. Blair. (eds), *Racism and Education: Structures and Strategies*. London: Sage

Young, V. (1970), Family and childhood in a southern Georgia community. *American Anthropologist* 72: 269-288

Younge, P. (1994) The Ex Generation., 15th November: 18-19 *The Voice*

Index